**DO NOT REMOVE
CARDS FROM POCKET**

INFLUENTIAL THEOLOGIANS ON WO/MAN

William E. Phipps

University Press
of America™

Copyright © 1981 by
University Press of America, Inc.™
P.O. Box 19101, Washington, D.C. 20036

Printed in the United States of America

ISBN: 0-8191-0880-4 (Perfect)
0-8191-1383-2 (Cloth)

Library of Congress Number: 79-5431

CONTENTS

PREFACE

Without the generous assistance of institutions and individuals this book could not have been written. I would like to thank in particular President Gordon Hermanson of Davis and Elkins College for again granting me a sabbatical leave to engage in research, and President James Laney of Emory University for inviting me to use the resources of one of the world's best theological libraries. My daughter Ruth has skillfully typed the manuscript for publication.

This book is dedicated to my unswerving friend, Dr. Thomas Richard Ross, Professor of History at Davis and Elkins College. Dick has continually encouraged my scholarly pursuits and has deepened my appreciation for democratic principles during our decades together on the same faculty. He combines with his excellent professional qualities a dedication to Christ like that of the apostle Paul and a devotion to spouse, Jean, like that of John Donne.

Elkins, W. Va.   Bill Phipps

INTRODUCTION

In both church and state, revolutions tend to end in repression from the new regime. Jesus was a revolutionary more unprecedented than those of the political and military type. The social upheaval that he inaugurated was fueled in no small part by his showing as much deference to women as to men. But his witness to sexual equality was generally unappreciated and suppressed in the church which he founded. Historian Charles Seltman, in his book Women in Antiquity, accurately concludes: "Jesus was a feminist to a degree far beyond that of his fellows and followers.... No other Western prophet, seer or would-be redeemer of humanity was so devoted to the feminine half of mankind."[1] How appropriate it is that the symbol both for Jesus and for woman is the same: a crossed upright. The cross-led crusades which they have launched have often foundered.

Jesus' doctrine of the full personhood of each sex was as old as the first chapter of Genesis. There it was declared many centuries before his birth that all men and women are created equal and that both sexes should have dominion over the earth. However, by Jesus' day, little attention had been given to putting that inspired sentiment into practice. One Israelite prophet, who was especially compassionate toward his wife, longed for the coming of the day of justice when the model for domestic and divine relationships would no longer be that of the male patriarch exercising dominion over his abject wife.[2] Jesus fleshed out a cardinal ideal of his Hebrew heritage, but it was too counter to conventional morality for even his closest disciples to accept completely.

Look at some of the revolutionary things that Jesus said and did which were not championed by his followers. He had the audacity to compare God to a woman—one in search of what was out of its proper place.[3] As a rabbi he was willing not only to teach women but to learn from them. After a discussion with an assertive Gentile woman he broadened the scope of his mission.[4] Jesus was

1

critical of the double standard of sexual morality and the traditional feminine stereotype.[5] Through example he encouraged women and men to step out of the constricting sex role boxes into which they had been placed. He sometimes did things not usually considered masculine--he wept with women, he washed men's feet, he identified with children.[6] Also, he became the advocate of women who were being trampled upon by unscrupulous landlords and by unjust judges.[7]

Indeed, Jesus' treatment of women, as recorded in the Gospels, attests to the very historicity of those accounts.[8] One of the best proofs that Jesus' teachings and actions were faithfully transmitted is that the Gospel record which the Christian community published does not reflect well the sexist culture in which the traditions were preserved. If the male dominated church had written pious fiction to reinforce its own accepted values, it would have portrayed the founder of Christianity as castigating "the weaker sex"[9] for deserting him at his crucifixion while his courageous male friends remained faithful. Its fabrication would have told of a disciplinarian who was harsh toward uppity women, and of a prude who separated himself from disreputable and sensuous women. A church-created-Jesus would have taught that Eve and her perverse daughters have caused man's downfall, but would have given assurance that "women will be saved through bearing children." He would have forbidden women "to teach or to have authority over men" and would have advised them to remain inconspicuous at public worship, leaving the praying up to the males.[10] If Jesus had articulated the sex role outlook that would prevail in the church at the end of the first century, he would have urged that a woman be trained as a "domestic worker"[11] to take care of the clothes, cleaning, cooking, and children in the home.

The New Testament Gospels are thus seen to be authentic reports of Jesus' radical feminism. But the apostolic church, to a lesser extent, and the post-apostolic church, to a greater extent, has repressed his democratic ideals. In fact, throughout most of church history there have been few women whose rightful dignity and theological abilities have been properly recognized. Even though the Gospel presents some of the most exalted teaching about the nature of God in the context of a woman's conversation with Jesus,[12] the church has done little until the past century to encourage women theologians. They have been as unusual as women surgeons or women philosophers in spite of the Gospel witness to woman's high status.

Redemption from the androcentric sin that is so endemic to humankind can not be quickly and effortlessly found. Yet the ugly weeds of sexist bigotry must be removed if the essential Gospel message is to flourish. So deeply rooted are these weeds that it is ineffective to attempt to purge them by slashing away at what is only above the surface in our generation. We need to uncover the historical roots of sexism and examine the personal lifestyles and the environmental soil which nourished its ancient and medieval growth. Then we may be able to destroy the weeds so that they will not continue to plague succeeding generations.

The five chapters that follow analyze in detail five influential Christians who were, to varying degrees, lacking in a Christlike concern for the opposite sex. There are two who came close, during the latter part of their lives, to expressing Jesus' outlook on male-female relationships. But three chapters describe men with perennial prejudices against women. They were not only literally unevangelical but also less appreciative of sexually active women than the ancient Jews were. Since the majority of Christians through the ages have also been antifeminists, the studies will reveal a rather representative viewpoint of both the leadership and the rank and file membership of the church.

Considering the myriad of persons who have had an impact on the church's view of male-female relationships, what has been the criteria for selecting these five? First, a few central figures have been passed over because I have dealt with them before. In previous publications I have examined, at least summarily, the

3

sexual attitudes of a number of significant theologians--Clement
of Alexandria, Origen, Tertullian, Bernard of Clairvaux, Thomas
Aquinas, Martin Luther, Huldreich Zwingli, John Calvin, and Soren
Kierkegaard. Also, I have already devoted books and articles to
the investigation of perspectives which Christians have had on the
sexuality of Jesus, contending that his historical lifestyle
should have paramount influence on Christian standards of male-
female behavior.[13] In this study I am interested in going beyond
previous studies and treating other important figures who have
been either altogether neglected or incompletely analyzed.

Second, included are only those men who have influenced many
millions of Christians, either positively or negatively. Billions
have been informed by the apostle Paul, for his writings are considered authoritative in both the Eastern and in the Western
Churches. That apostle, along with his disciple Luke, wrote more
than half of the New Testament and the two have a great deal to say
about the status of women in the church. Jerome and Augustine are
the two pivotal personalities in early Latin Christianity. Since
most Christians across the centuries and around the world have
called themselves Catholics, their influence has been far reaching.
In addition, Augustine's doctrines of sin and salvation have been
widely endorsed by Protestant leaders. John Knox and John Donne,
as other Reformation leaders, have an appeal that is more national
and denominational. Yet, even though they lack the international
stature of some of the church fathers, they are among the more
outstanding figures in the history of the Church of Scotland and
Church of England. Those British churches have, in turn, had the
most effect on North American religious developments.

Third, theologians who have lived since the age of the Reformation have not been considered. The multi-branching of Christianity
during the past several centuries has diminished the breadth of
influence that individual leaders have had. Mary Baker Eddy, for
example, developed a distinctive theology that has significance for
male-female relationships, but her Christian Science religion has

4

never had a mass appeal. There are a few twentieth century theologians, such as Karl Barth and Paul Tillich, who are now influential in several branches of the church, but it is too early to discern how abiding their influence will be.

Fourth, in order to keep this probe into the many centuries of church history from becoming unwieldy, an effort has been made to limit the centuries under investigation. Three periods have been selected in which a new culture was being born with all the accompanying travail. Those cultures are those of the earliest church, when Christianity was separating from mother Judaism, the medieval, when institutional Christianity was replacing the Roman empire, and the modern, when secular society became divorced from religious domination. By taking these three cross-sectional slices into Western history a great deal will be disclosed about the entire sweep of Christianity vis à vis wo/man.

Starting with Paul provides some unity to this study, for he was esteemed by all the rest, no matter how much they differed with one another in their interpretations of what he wrote. Jerome and Augustine thought of Paul as a fellow ascetic who eschewed women but Knox and Donne viewed the apostle as one who endorsed marital intimacy. All four of Paul's admirers became, as their mentor, preachers and pastors, and, like him, goaded by and repentant of their youthful excesses. Most of them acknowledged that they had had an unbridled lust for women and prayed that God would transform their horniness into holiness. However, the painful "prick" that troubled the young Paul resulted not from philandering but from his persecution of Christians.[14] After each man took Christianity seriously there was a pronounced vocational shift: Paul the rabbi became an apostle; Jerome the classicist became a biblicist; Augustine the rhetorician became a bishop; Knox the lawyer-cleric became a Protestant minister; Donne the bureaucrat became a cathedral dean.

Jerome provides a bridge for passing from the ancient Mediterrean to medieval Europe. He was as cosmopolitan as Paul, only

5

he moved eastward in the latter part of his life from Rome to Palestine. Both Jerome and Augustine drank deeply from the springs of monasticism in fourth century North Africa. Those two men did more than any others to mold the millennium of medieval Christianity. Jerome drew on his phenomenal linguistic talent to translate and interpret Scriptures. Augustine's genius lay more in relating the prevailing Greco-Roman philosophies to Christian doctrine. Jerome was as pugnacious as Knox--both mercilessly stabbed with their pens those whom they resented. While Jerome's contentions were usually with fellow monks, Knox assailed Catholic queens. Jerome and Knox, unlike the rest, were not seminal theologians, so little of significant doctrinal formulation can be found in their writings. Finally, Jerome and Donne were bibliophiles, being among the most widely read persons of their times. Both were masters of satirical wit.

Even though three of the five men who will be studied are commonly referred to by the designation of "saint," this title has been dropped. Its omission should not be interpreted as a lack of respect for Paul, Jerome, and Augustine, but as an honoring of the way the term saint (hagios) was first used in Christianity. Paul never used the term in the singular for he did not intend that it should designate the exemplary devoutness of particular individuals. He applied hagios to Christians generally, so he would probably have protested vigorously to its later discriminatory usage. Beginning with the medieval church, the hierarchy has invidiously attempted to segregate those with summa cum laude piety from hoi polloi Christians. But, to take an example, what qualities of exceptional holiness distinguish priest Jerome from priest John Donne?

Ascriptions of devoutness have also been detrimental to honest biographical study. Hagiographers, who are more interested in gilding imaginary halos than in exposing real foibles, have not heeded Paul's advice. He exhorted the saints of Thessalonica to combine respect with scrutiny in dealing with those who are considered inspired spokesmen. "Test everything," he cautioned, "hold fast what is good."[15] The apostle here vindicates the right and duty of critical judgment, which is as basic to intelligent religion as to sound science. Albert Schweitzer, one of the great minds of this century, has written: "Paul is the patron saint of thought in Christianity. And all those who think to serve the faith in Jesus by destroying freedom of thought would do well to keep out of his way."[16] In the chapters ahead we will attempt to test Paul and all the other theologians against the Magna Charta of feminism which was announced in the imago dei passage of Genesis and fully put into practice by Jesus.

NOTES

1. Charles Seltman, Women in Antiquity (London, 1957), pp. 148-149.

2. Hosea 2:16, 19.

3. Luke 15:8-10.

4. Mark 7:24-30.

5. Cf. John 8:2-11; Luke 10:38-42.

6. Cf. Luke 18:15-17; John 11:35; 13:4-5.

7. Mark 12:40; Luke 18:2-5.

8. Cf. Charles Moule, The Phenomenon of the New Testament (London, 1967), pp. 63-64.

9. 1 Peter 3:7.

10. 1 Tim. 2:8-15.

11. Titus 2:5.

12. John 4:7-26.

13. William E. Phipps, Was Jesus Married? The Distortion of Sexuality in the Christian Tradition (New York, 1970--reprinted by University Microfilms, Ann Arbor, Mich.); The Sexuality of Jesus: Theological and Literary Perspectives (New York, 1973-- republished as Did Jesus Love? by Harper and Row, 1979.)

14. Acts 26:14.

15. 1 Thess. 5:21.

16. Albert Schweitzer, The Mysticism of Paul the Apostle (New York, 1960), p. 377.

CHAPTER 1
PAUL AND FEMINISM

The apostle Paul is now regarded as the source of both anti-
feminism and feminism in the Christian tradition. This bewildering
situation can be illustrated by sampling remarks of some twentieth
century interpreters. Playwright George Bernard Shaw stated that
the apostle made himself "the eternal enemy of woman" by insisting
"that a wife should be rather a slave than a partner."[1] More
recently philogynist Elizabeth Davis has expressed this judgment:
"Paul's antifeminism amounted to an active phobia of all things female." She goes on to speak of his "rabid misogyny."[2]

Contemptuous utterances such as these have brought forth
spirited responses from some New Testament scholars. Oxford don
G. B. Caird has made this scathing observation: "Of all the
prejudices and half-truths which together comprise the biblical
semiliteracy of the man in the street, none is more firmly held
than the belief that Paul was the founder of an agelong conspiracy
to deny women their rights." Caird has written an article in which
he argues "that this prevalent disparagement is almost the exact
antithesis of the truth."[3] There have also been some in the
United States who have recently come to Paul's defense. Robin
Scroggs evidently regards Paul as even more of a feminist than
Jesus. This is the thesis that Scroggs attempts to defend: "Paul
is, so far from being a chauvinist, the only certain and consis-
tent spokesman for the liberation and equality of women in the
New Testament."[4] Derwood Smith also published an essay which tries
to defend a similar position. He states: "Paul, more than any
other known Christian in the mainstream of the early church, stands
as the radical advocate of the complete liberation of woman."[5]

What accounts for this polarization of interpretations? Is
it that only biblical specialists have ability to read Paul's letters
properly? Or do they have vested interests in making the area of
their expertise appealing to human rights advocates? What basis

9

does either side have for its outspoken judgment? We shall examine, in historical order, four passages from Paul's letters that both groups use to support their interpretations.

1 Corinthians 7:1-5

The opening verse of 1 Corinthians 7 contains this brash sentence: "It is good for a man not to touch a woman." This was a favorite verse for the ascetic church fathers. Tertullian drew this implication from Paul's words: "It follows that it is evil to have contact with a woman; for nothing is contrary to good except evil."[6] The influence of Tertullian can be detected in Jerome's more elaborate treatment. That fourth century monk wrote:

> If "it is good for a man not to touch a woman," it is bad for him to touch one: for there is no opposite to goodness but badness....Notice the apostle's prudence. He did not say, "It is good for a man not to have a wife" but "It is good for a man not to touch a woman"--as though there were danger even in the touch....He who touches fire is instantly burned.... Joseph, because the Egyptian woman wished to touch him, fled from her hands, and, as if he had been bitten by a mad dog and feared the spreading poison, threw away the cloak which she had touched.[7]

Augustine, writing about the same time as Jerome, honored "It is good for a man not to touch a woman" as the very word of God--its source is a "voice from the clouds."[8] No reference is made to the fact that the words were written by Paul and in a passage where he stresses that he is giving his personal opinion.

There are a number of modern New Testament scholars who cite 1 Cor. 7:1 as evidence of Paul's sexual asceticism.[9] For example, Johannes Weiss has written: "Paul actually considers sexual intercourse as something which draws man from God and is degrading to him: 'It is good for a man not to touch a woman.' This is his ideal."[10] Also, in the influential Interpreter's Bible, Clarence Craig's comment on this verse presumes that Paul reversed the normative Old Testament outlook on marriage. That exegete draws this contrast: "In Gen. 2:18 we read, 'It is not good that man should be alone.' Paul thought that the opposite was true."[11]

10

Some twentieth century Pauline scholars in several countries
have claimed that the negative evaluation of sexual intercourse in
1 Cor. 7:1 is not Paul's personal judgment but the viewpoint of
some ascetic Corinthians.[12] David Smith, for instance, holds that
Paul began his discussion of marriage in 1 Cor. 7 by quoting a
position which he rejected.[13] E. W. Hunt provides this paraphrase
of verse 1: "I am now turning to the particular matters which you
mention in your letter to me. You say, 'The proper course for a
man is to discontinue sexual intercourse with his wife.'"[14]

There are stylistic and contextual reasons for regarding "It
is good for a man not to touch a woman" as a position which Paul
opposed. With respect to letter writing style, the apostle devoted
much of 1 Corinthians to replying to various problems on which
his advice was solicited. Beginning with 1 Cor. 7:1 he introduced
his response to six different matters by the standard formula,
peri de ("now concerning").[15] Before giving his advice Paul
sometimes quoted a slogan which he found objectionable in the
communication received from those he was addressing.[16] 1 Cor. 8:1,
for instance, is properly punctuated thus: "Now concerning food
offered to idols: we know that 'we all have knowledge.'" It is
puzzling that modern translators generally place quotation marks
around that Corinthian saying but do not do so with 1 Cor. 7:1
where the style is quite similar.[17]

Contextual reasons are even more compelling than the stylistic
reasons for judging "It is good for a man not to touch a woman" to
be contrary to Paul's own position. In the paragraph immediately
before 1 Cor. 7:1, Paul appeals to the Genesis 2 account of creation which affirms that it is good for a man to become one flesh
with a woman. He draws an analogy between sexual union and the
union of the Christian with Christ. It would also violate the
context of what follows 1 Cor. 7:1 to presume that Paul's position
was stated in that verse. In verses two and five he recommends
marital intercourse as a curb against prostitution and adultery.
In verses three and four he clearly affirms that both wives and

11

husbands have equal conjugal rights and obligations.

Paul, in recognizing that both spouses have sexual urges that need satisfying, shows an understanding that has been rare in history. Sex researchers William Masters and Virginia Johnson demonstrate that prior to our modern era "women were trained to be sexual marionettes."[18] One notable exception was the medieval Wife of Bath who acted on her understanding of Paul's position. She has this to say regarding her privileges and her spouse's duty:

> I have the power duringe al my lyf
> Up-on his propre body, and noght he.
> Right thus th' apostel tolde it un-to me; [19]
> And bad our housbondes for to love us weel.

In our present day Eleanor McLaughlin notes that the outlook which Paul expresses here is "a truly revolutionary concept that decreed a genuine reciprocity in the sexual relationship."[20]

The affirmation of sexual equality in the opening paragraph of 1 Corinthians 7 sets the tone for Paul's treatment of divorce in verses 10-16. Paul followed Jesus in rejecting Judaism's double standard of divorce,[21] and consequently he presumed that a wife had as much right as the husband to initiate divorce. The apostle stressed that the bond of matrimony places similar responsibilities upon each partner. Wayne Meeks has demonstrated that this mutuality between the sexes which Paul here advocates "is virtually unparalleled in Jewish or pagan society of the time."[22]

1 Corinthians 11:3-12

This difficult passage contains one verse which is cited by those who see Paul as a feminist and another verse which proves to others that he was an antifeminist. In verse five the apostle acknowledges that women could prophesy in public worship. He gave this role of inspired preaching a high status, second only to apostleship.[23] Paul came out of a tradition that highly honored female prophets such as Miriam, Deborah, and Huldah.[24] Songs attributed to two of these prophetesses are in the oldest stratum of biblical literature. By recognizing that prophetic charisma could be found in either sex, Paul is in harmony with what Luke

12

records of the early church.[25]

In light of this openness to women speaking, why did Paul, in his discussion of glossolalia, state that "women should keep silence"?[26] Since he had already, in the same letter, stated that women could prophesy in church, it is reasonable to assume that he was not, in 1 Corinthians 14, inconsistently rejecting women preachers. The context of that chapter shows that Paul was troubled that "speaking in tongues" could transform edifying worship into meaningless babble. In his advocacy for order he recommended to all--both men and women--that each person should keep silent while others are speaking. Perhaps there had been called to Paul's attention that women had been disruptive during community worship, and therefore he directed some remarks to them. Women in the Greek culture found ecstatic religious activities especially appealing because they provided an outlet for frustrations that had been socially repressed.[27] Paul's criticism of some noisy women in Corinth should not be used to prove that he believed in female inferiority any more than 1 Cor. 7:4 ("The husband does not rule over his own body, but his wife does.") should be ripped out of its context to prove that he advocated matriarchy.

Those who think Paul was an antifeminist cite 1 Cor. 11:7: "Man (aner, a male person)...is the image and glory of God, but woman is the glory of man." Here the apostle greatly distorts the creation account of Gen. 1:27 which states: "God created humankind (adam, Hebrew; anthropos, Greek) in his own image;...male and female he created them." Paul made the commonplace error of presuming that the generic term for man in Genesis referred only to the male portion of humanity, even though the verse to which he alluded explicitly points out that both sexes are made in the divine likeness.

Throughout church history those who have held that woman is inferior to man have opted for Paul's perverse interpretation of Gen. 1:27. In the fourth century Biship Cyril of Alexandria commented: "Woman is in man's likeness, image of an image, and glory

of glory."[28] Aquinas, following Augustine, articulated the prevailing medieval position in declaring that "the image of God is
found in man, and not in woman, for man is the beginning and end
of woman."[29] In the present generation Jesuit Fernand Prat cham-
pions the Pauline interpretation when he claims that man is "the
direct reflection of divine majesty" whereas woman is like a reflection of a reflection.[30]

Male interpreters in the Protestant as well as in the Catholic
tradition have generally preferred the imago dei interpretation of
1 Cor. 11 to that of Gen. 1. John Milton asserted that Gen. 1:27
is unclear on the status of woman, but "Paul ends the controversie
by explaining that woman is not primary and immediately the image
of God." Believing that woman is "an inferiour sexe,"[31] he describes the religious standing of Adam and Eve thus: "Hee for God
only, shee for God in him."[32] Karl Barth is more subtle in rejecting sexual equality on the authority of Paul. He holds that the
proper relation of man to woman is a hierarchical one. It is part
of the divine order, he contends, for woman to see herself in proper "sequence," acknowledging man as her leader.[33]

Romans 16

The concluding chapter of Paul's magnum opus is another source
for opposite interpretations of the apostle's outlook on women.
John Knox, a founder of Scottish Presbyterianism, was appreciative
of an interpretation of Rom. 16:13 which had been attri uted to
Bishop Ambrose. That verse reads: "Greet Rufus, eminent in the
Lord, also his mother and mine." Ambrose held that Rufus was
named first to show that he had superiority over his mother. John
Knox, in his First Blast of the Trumpet against the Monstrous
Regiment of Women, concluded from this interpretation by a church
father that "It is plaine that the administration of the grace of
God is denied to all women."[34] What seems more plain is that Knox,
in combating sixteenth century female monarchs, was desperate in
his search for some biblical verse that would give sanction to his
rabid prejudice against women rulers. The King James Version seems

to show the influence of John Knox, for, without textual basis, it is demeaning to some of the women mentioned in Romans 16. After it refers to Phoebe as a "servant" (diakonos) and a "succourer" (prostatis), it calls Priscilla a "helper" (sunergos).

During the past generation New Testament scholars have viewed Rom. 16 quite differently. E. F. Scott states that the chapter reveals "a church in which women played a leading part, as they no doubt did in all the churches which Paul had founded."[35] Arthur Nock appeals to this chapter in support of his judgment that "Paul had no objection to women holding administrative offices and welcomed their activities."[36] Living prior to the development of church hierarchy, it appears that the apostle encouraged any talented person to assume a responsible role in the missionary enterprise. He believed that each man or woman who had been touched by God's grace (charis) had a gift (charisma) that should be utilized.

An analysis of Romans 16 discloses that many women are commended for their courage, hard work, friendship, and, in some cases, leadership. The first person to be mentioned is Phoebe, who was probably entrusted to be the courier for the important Romans letter.[37] One of the titles she is given is diakonos, a Greek term which is usually rendered "minister" in English translations of the New Testament. Paul had used diakonos in the preceding chapter to refer to the important roles that he and Christ had in the church.

There has been great reluctance to translate diakonos consistently. In the King James Version diakonos is translated eighteen times as "minister" is Paul's letters and as "servant" only in reference to a woman. The Moffatt translation and the Revised Standard Version do acknowledge that Phoebe held office by calling her a "deaconess." However, Paul does not give diakonos a feminine ending, so there is no basis for presuming that Phoebe is the first to be mentioned of a separate female order. The same term diakonos is used to refer to a government ruler in Rom 13:4, and in Phil. 1:1

the term is in tandem with the office of bishop. It is also used
in 1 Cor. 3:5, but no translation of that verse reads like this:
"What then is Apollos? What is Paul? Deacons through whom you
believed." It is apparent that deliberate attempts have been made
over the centuries to diminish Phoebe's role as minister by placing
her in a separate subordinate order, or in no order at all. Sexual
discrimination is notable in The Living Bible which destroys the
original connotation of diakonos by this so-called paraphrase:
"Phoebe, a dear Christian woman." However, in reference to Paul
and Timothy in 2 Cor. 6:4, this publication does not read "we are
dear Christian men" but, more properly, "we are true ministers
(diakonoi) of God."

Due to Paul's approval of women ministers, they were afforded
high status in the early church.[38] Origen asserted that Rom. 16
gave apostolic authority for recognizing women ministers in the
church.[39] Pliny, the Roman governor of Asia, in a Latin letter
written to Emperor Trajan in 112 A. D., tells of torturing two
women whom Christians called "ministers" (ministrae).[40]

The other title which Paul gave Phoebe is prostatis. It
literally means "one who stands over" and is associated with high
authority. In the classical Greek lexicon by Liddell and Scott,
the definitions given for prostatis are: "a front-rank man," "a
chief, especially of a party," and "a protector, guard, champion."
The noun does not occur elsewhere in the New Testament but it is
used in a first century letter to refer to Christ's role as
guardian and protector.[41] In the Septuagint it refers to admin-
istrators and governors.[42] Prostatis is virtually equivalent to
episkopos, overseer, which designates the office of bishop in the
New Testament. The verbal form proistemi means "to rule" or "to
manage" in Paul's letters.[43] Thus, translations of prostatis as
"helper" (Revised Standard Version) or as "good friend" (New
English Bible) in Rom 16:2 are obviously degrading. It seems that
Phoebe was appointed by Paul to be a supervisory minister. She
was given authority, for Paul asks the letter recipients to "help

16

her with anything she needs."

Paul next greets a married couple, mentioning the wife Priscilla before her husband Aquila. He calls them his co-workers (sunergoi), the same term he uses elsewhere to refer to such trusted companions as Timothy, Titus, and Luke.[44] Priscilla's status was at least as high as that of the Philippian sunergoi to whom Paul gave this tribute: "They have labored side by side with me in the gospel."[45] When Luke states that Priscilla and her husband "expounded" the way of God, he uses the same verb as in describing the manner in which Paul taught in Rome.[46]

In 1977 the Vatican issued a declaration "On the Ordination of Women to the Ministerial Priesthood" which states that "Paul did not make use of women's help to the extent of entrusting them with the public function of solemnly proclaiming the Gospel." The basis given for this assertion is that Paul called women such as Priscilla, Christian co-workers, but the phrase "co-worker of God" in 1 Cor. 3:9 and in 1 Thess. 3:2 "is reserved for Apollos, Timothy, and Paul himself."[47] This invidious interpretation can be credited for novelty but not for soundness.

Luke does not indicate that Priscilla and Aquila were converted to Christianity by Paul, so it can be presumed that they were Christians in Rome before being exiled to Corinth.[48] It could well be that they were among the founders of the church in Rome. Since Paul wrote to that church prior to visiting it, the Christian community in Rome must have been initiated by someone else. Perhaps it was established two decades earlier by some Jews from the Diaspora who are mentioned as having been present for the first Christian Pentecost in Jerusalem. Aquila, a Jew, was a native of Pontus, and Luke states that visitors from that place were Pentecost witnesses.[49] It is more likely that Priscilla and her husband started the church at Rome than Peter, the traditional founder, who did not think of himself as an apostle to the Gentiles.[50]

Due to Paul's recognition of Priscilla's abilities, she may have written the letter to the Hebrews. If so, she has the singular distinction of being not only the only known female biblical writer but also the only woman whose book has survived from the classical era.[51] Adolf Harnack, a distinguished German church historian, argued that Priscilla was the probable author of Hebrews but that her name was obliterated from the now anonymous letter because of her sex.[52] Harnack's opinion has been defended by Arthur Peake, an outstanding British exegete.[53] It is at least as plausible to think that Hebrews was written by Priscilla as to accept Luther's assumption that the letter was written by Apollos, whom Priscilla instructed in theology. Lee Starr has accepted Harnack's position and has given thirteen arguments in favor of Priscilla's authorship.[54]

The third woman of special significance whom Paul greets in Romans 16 is named along with Andronicus in verse 7. She is given either the name of Julia of Junia in the earliest manuscripts. It is likely that she and Andronicus were married. Paul states that the two were "outstanding apostles,"[55] that they were fellow Jews, that they became Christians before his conversion, and that they had been imprisoned with him. Paul believed that apostles were distinguished from other Christian missionaries by having received a vision of the resurrected Jesus. Julia, like James the brother of Jesus, was evidently called an apostle because of that experience.[56]

Although most churchmen across the centuries have been unwilling to admit that a woman could have been accorded the highest rank and honor in the church, some patristic commentators have acknowledged that she was an apostle.[57] Chrysostom exclaimed: "How great was the devotion of this woman that she should be counted worthy of the title apostle!"[58] Modern biblical translators have not been nearly as charitable as that Greek father, for most of them presume that Andronicus' companion must have been a male and thus they fabricate for Iounia a masculine ending.

However, their creation, _Iounias_, although masculine in form, is not a name found elsewhere in ancient records. Contemporary translators who make this name error have even less excuse because only they are aware of the reading of a text that has been recently discovered. According to the Chester Beatty papyrus, Julia is the name of the first female apostle on record.

Ephesians 5:21-33

Unlike the other letters that have been considered in this chapter, there is considerable dispute among contemporary scholars over the authorship of Ephesians. Two recent scholars, after weighing this question thoroughly, have concluded that the arguments in favor of regarding Paul as the author are stronger than those against.[59] Since there is general agreement that the letter contains Pauline positions even if it might have been written by one of Paul's disciples, the question of authorship is not a significant one.

Often feminists who are disgusted with Paul's alleged anti-feminism focus on selected verses pertaining to male-female relationships in the Ephesian letter. Here is the way John Stuart Mill misunderstood that letter: "We are told that St. Paul said, 'Wives, obey your husbands'; but he also said, 'Slaves, obey your masters.'"[60] It is surprising that Mill, famous for his inductive method, did not examine what Paul actually said. The verb "obey" (hupakouo) is used by Paul to refer to the proper relationship of slaves to masters and of children to parents,[61] but he never used it to refer to a wife's relation to her husband. Typical of many, Mill uncritically relied on the commonplace English interpretation, such as the one given centuries earlier by Puritan theologian Paul Bayne. His commentary on Eph. 5:21 gives illustrations of ways in which a wife ought to express "obedience." "If a man should go to blows she must endure with patience." Again, "The man has a negative voice; if he say no, all must be dashed."[62] It appears that Bayne expected a wife to respond like a cringing, docile dog.

Simone De Beauvoir also wrests the Ephesian passage under consideration to support her contention that Paul was "savagely antifeminist."[63] She quotes only verses that treat a wife's duty, omitting those verses that stress a husband's reciprocal duty. Actually the apostle follows three verses (22-24) pertaining to the former with twice as many verses (25-30) pertaining to the latter. An even more outspoken criticism has recently been raised by theologian Rosemary Ruether. This is her amazing accusation: "The author of the Epistle to the Ephesians, who ratified a subjection of wives to husbands modeled on the subjugation of the creature to God, established a sexist idolatry in the heart of Christian symbolism that allowed males to play God in relation to subjected women."[64]

There are other women who are sure that Paul was not a feminist and admire him for his stance. Marabel Morgan, the author of the best-seller Total Woman, quotes Eph. 5:22, "Wives submit yourselves to your husbands as to the Lord," and comments: "God planned for woman to be under her husband's rule....It is only when a woman surrenders her life to her husband, reveres and worships him, and is willing to serve him, that she becomes really beautiful to him."[65] Similarly Judith Miles responds to Eph. 5:22 by testifying: "I was to treat my own human husband as though he were the Lord.... Would I remind the Lord that he was not driving prudently? Would I ever be in judgment over my Lord, over his taste, his opinions, or his actions? I was stunned--stunned into a new kind of submission."[66] "Total" wives who participate in this idolatry have a chronological outlook different from that of orthodox Christianity, for Anno Domini, the year of the advent of their Lord and Master, is, in effect, the year of their wedding.

Pioneer feminist Sarah Grimke pointed out as long ago as 1837 that it is perverse to read Eph. 5:22 out of context. In Greek the verse has no verb and is grammatically dependent upon the preceding verse which reads, "Submit yourself to one another out of reverence for Christ." Grimke shows that in the paragraph beginning

20

with Eph. 5:21 Paul first introduces his principle of voluntary mutual submission and then, in turn, addresses himself to wives and to husbands. Grimke was especially vexed by Puritan John Milton who professed to accept the biblical standard for human relationships, yet presumed blind obedience to be woman's proper relationship to man. Milton's Eve says to Adam:

> My Author and Disposer, what thou bidst,
> Unargu'd I obey; so God ordains,
> God is thy Law, thou mine: to know no more,
> Is woman's happiest knowledge and her praise. [67]

Grimke retorts: "This much admired sentimental nonsense is fraught with absurdity and wickedness. If it were true, the commandment of Jehovah should have run thus: Man shall have no other gods before me, and woman shall have no other gods before man."[68]

Paul's outlook on marriage may be clarified by contrasting it with two other basic patterns. First, there is the dominant spouse over submissive spouse variety. This might be called a 70-30 relationship, for one partner obtains the greater percentage of credit for initiative and important decisions. Traditionally, in most cultures, the husband has been the primary decision-maker. However, even in a patriarchal society some clever wives--such as Rebekah--manipulate their husbands and de facto call the main signals, so that the male primacy is more honorific than actual.

Second, there is the egalitarian type. Each spouse presumes that he or she has approximately the same role competence, whether it be breadmaking or breadwinning. In this 50-50 deal there is often little bending of individual self-interest or tolerance of diversity. Each tends to be highly defensive of her or his rights and gives utmost attention to seeing that they not be trampled upon. This relationship frequently stimulates fussing characteristic of siblings over the limits of each person's share of the work, with neither giving way to the other. There is little "acceptance of vulnerability," a dimension which Masters and Johnson say is much needed in marriage.[69]

21

Third, there is the mutual dominance-submissive variety. To use existential mathematics, this is a 70-70 proposition. The beatitude for this realtionship is: Happy are those who focus on the well-being of the other. The partners have freely placed themselves under the power of one another. As a biblical bride put it, "My beloved is mine and I am his."[70]

Paul would agree with those feminists who say that unilateral dependence in marriage is unhealthy. But he would point out that the alternative need not be an independence of husband and wife, which some now refer to as contract marriage. Paul composed a declaration of interdependence that aims at oneness. The arithmetic of independence is $1+1=2$, whereas the arithmetic of interdependence is $1 \times 1 = 1$. When there is complementarity each partner is both submissive and superior. In spite of Mill's criticism of Paul's view of marriage, the two shared a common ideal. The excellent marriage, Mill believed, is one in which there is "reciprocal superiority." In such a relationship "each can enjoy the luxury of looking up to the other, and can have alternately the pleasure of leading and of being led in the path of development."[71]

An intriguing parallel between marital, ecclesiastical, and bodily interdependence is occasionally drawn by Paul. He utilizes this triple analogy: husband is to wife as Christ is to church as head is to body. Since each part is indispensable to the vital functioning of the whole, it is futile to argue, for example, over whether what is above the neck is more valuable than what is below. In one of the earliest Protestant expositions of Eph. 5:21-33, Swiss Reformer Henry Bullinger writes: "As there is great unity and mutual love among the parts of a man's body, so ought there to be also between those that are married. Every member helps another: they are sorry and merry together; there is not one that checks and upbraids another; everyone has his place and office in the body and does his duty without grudging: even so must it be between husband and wife."[72]

Jesus, the Christ, was not an authoritarian "head" who preferred those whose aim was "not to reason why" but "to do and die." The picture that the New Testament paints of him is not that of a dictatorial ruler who recruited uncritical lackeys as disciples. J. H. Yoder points out that Jesus introduced a "revolutionary subordination" principle that was accepted by Paul.[73] The transvaluation of values to which Jesus was devoted is summed up in these words to his disciples: "You know that pagan rulers lord it over their subjects and exercise tyrannical power. But it shall not be so among you....For even the Son of Man came not to be served but to serve."[74] According to the Gospel of John, Jesus preferred to call his disciples friends rather than servants, and it was he who washed their feet.[75] Thus Paul writes to the Philippian church: "Do not act for selfish ends or from vanity, but modestly treat one another as your superiors." He then presents as a behavioral model Jesus, who "emptied himself" and became a humble servant.[76]

Paul was hopeful that spouses would re-present to one another God's self-giving Incarnation. "Be kind to one another," the apostle exhorts the Ephesians, "tenderhearted, forgiving one another, as God in Christ forgave you."[77] Then, in the same chapter where Paul discusses marital responsibilities, he counsels, "Walk in love as Christ loved us and gave himself for us."[78] That love involved total commitment and complete vulnerability. This treatment of the Christ is to church as husband is to wife parallel can well be concluded by Markus Barth's comments:

> In Eph. 5:22-33, the bossy husband who treats his wife with contempt receives much longer and much more incisive commands and advice than the wife. The obvious presupposition is that there were husbands who only used, clothed, fed and promenaded their wives--much as farmers do their prize cows at a fair. Such husbands are called to be heads of their wives by loving them with a love that responds and corresponds to Christ's love....The submission to, and respect for, the husband, to which the wife is specifically admonished is by no means the submissiveness of a pussy cat or a crouching dog....Paul is thinking of a voluntary, free, joyful, and thankful partnership, as the analogy of the relationship of the Church to Christ shows.[79]

23

In the Ephesian passage under consideration Paul approached the love of spouse from an ethical as well as from a Christological approach. The apostle, like Jesus, regarded "Love your neighbor as you love yourself" as the epitome of Jewish ethics.[80] In his parable of the Good Samaritan, Jesus suggested that "neighbor" should be defined so as to include the distant foreigner.[81] In his discussion of marriage in the Ephesian letter Paul urged that the agape principle be applied to the nearest neighbor, one's spouse.

Paul was the first of those few Christian leaders who have explicitly recognized that one of Jesus' "great commandments" implies that self-love can be a good thing. Augustine later followed up on the apostle's assessment of self-love, even though he did not apply it to the marital relationship. Augustine states:

> The apostle says truly, "No man ever hated his own flesh."... That he does love himself, and does desire to do good to himself, nobody but a fool would doubt. Yet he must be instructed regarding how he should love his body so that he may care for it wisely and within due limits....When it is said, "You shall love your neighbor as yourself," it at once becomes evident that our love for ourselves has not been overlooked.[82]

It has been mainly non-Christian ethicists who have encouraged self-love. The first was Aristotle who attempted to rescue the concept from an exclusively bad connotation. "Those who use 'self-love' as a term of reproach," he observed, "ascribe the epithet to people who grasp for themselves more than their shave of wealth, honors, and bodily pleasures." But Aristotle offered this reinterpretation: "If anyone were always concerned to take the lead in acting justly or with self-control, or in accordance with any of the other virtues, and in general were always trying to secure for himself the honorable course of action, nobody would stigmatize him as 'a self-lover.' Yet such a person would seem more than others a lover of self." Aristotle believed that "all the affectionate feelings of a person for others are an extension of his feelings for himself."[83] Psychoanalyst Erich Fromm has demonstrated that persons who despise themselves are incapable of loving

24

others.[84] Self-hatred is the route to suicide but genuine self-affirmation is a moral necessity. Self-love should not be confused with selfishness.

In what follows an attempt will be made to apply love of myself to love of my spouse. It is, in effect, simply working out some implications of the Golden Rule--namely, what is involved in treating others as one desires to be treated. After examining some physical and emotional concerns, focus will be given to matters that are more intellectual and spiritual. How do I love myself? "Let me count the ways."

Love of Self

--Paul wrote: "No man ever hates his own flesh, but feeds and cherishes it."[85] I am eager that my stomach receives food that I find especially tasty--such as thick gravy prepared by my mother's recipe. Also, I daily cherish my appearance as I shave.

--Another way I love myself is in understanding the way in which my physiological condition affects my disposition and in knowing how to relieve the situation. When I am fatigued I am concerned that my home be quiet so that my body can be given its well-deserved rest. When I am feisty I expect the family to tolerate, even if

Love of Spouse

--"Even so," wrote Paul, "Husbands should love their wives as their own bodies."[86] I should cultivate a taste for foods that my wife finds delectable--such as the gingerbread that her family has always associated with Christmas. Her occasional use of mirrors should be evaluated as good grooming, not as vanity.

--Accordingly, I should be sensitive to the way strenuous activity and gynecological periods affect moods. Recognizing that individuals differ in sleep requirements I should be accepting of my spouse's propensity to snooze late in the morning. There is a time to dance and a time to embrace. I should realize that satisfying

25

Love of Self

they cannot enjoy, my lusty
singing and horsing around.
Frequently I have a sexual
urge which I want to relieve
under optimum conditions. I
desire a partner who will
passionately stroke my whole
body.

--I admire my physique even
though others may not find it
attractive. My mother liked
my dimpled cheeks and the large
hairy mole on my forehead which
she called my "beauty spot."
Understandably I am also fond
of these physiognomic
eccentricities. The middle-
age metamorphosis of my teeth,
hair, and skin does not diminish
the way I cherish my appearance. As regards athletic
abilities, my prowess at sports
never won a prize but I am
happy to exchange that record
for no broken bones or torn
ligaments.

--I think that it is often
cathartic to express my anger
when irritated, rather than to
permit resentments to build
up. However, Paul wisely

Love of Spouse

intercourse is more than link-
ing loins and stimulating orgasms. A lover should be like
that biblical bridegroom who
was enthralled by the feet,
thighs, navel, breasts, neck,
lips, nose, eyes, and hair of
his beloved.[87]

--In other ages and cultures
my spouse's pearlike proportions
might have won a beauty con-
test, but they do not measure
up to the contemporary American dream. However, I find
her as lovely as her demitasse
china which features petite
cups set in harmonizing saucers.
Sometimes I am envious of her
well-padded buttocks as I realize that she, unlike myself,
can sit comfortably for hours
on a hard seat. Geriatric
bulges and wrinkles will not
cause my appreciation for her
distinctive body to atrophy.

--It is also unhealthy for my
wife to bottle up tensions that
may distill into gall. Unlike
anger, Paul regarded bitterness
as only a vice.[89] Hence, he

26

Love of Self

advised that blowing off emotional pressure should be for a very limited time and that one should not "let the sun go down" on a quarrel.[88] A verbal duel is transposed into a vibrant duet when a making-up follows in the wake of a falling-out.

--I love the intellectual and spiritual dimensions of myself even more than the physical and emotional aspects. Nothing intrigues me more than entertaining unconventional notions and tossing them out for discussion. I delight in communicating ideas, even while realizing that most will be judged to be more crazy than creative. It is my hope that others will respect my tentative viewpoints by taking time to articulate frank criticisms. Following Paul's advice, I strive to have a sensible estimation of my capabilities-- not thinking of myself too highly or too lowly.[92]

Love of Spouse

counselled, "Love your wives and be not bitter."[90] Reconciliation of those alienated is basic to all facet's of Paul's gospel.[91] Loss of temper might be more infrequent if we were more appreciative of one another's accomplishments.

--I should cultivate the art of asking what my wife is thinking and then of listening with total concentration to what is being shared. She should contribute her mild and wild ideas to the decisionmaking process of the family, and I owe it to her to respond candidly and rationally. After hearing what appears to her to be the truth on an issue I should--to use a lovely phrase of Paul--"speak the truth in love."[93] Out of exchanging playful and serious comments, common understandings and joint plans for action can be reached.

Love of Self

--I find that Paul's famous ode to love in 1 Corinthians 13 expresses some qualities of my self-love. I am very patient with myself because of the hope that I have for self improvement. Hence, I am prone to believe the best about myself and am cautious in exposing my poor performance to the public. For example, when others taunt me for my absent-mindedness, I come to my defense by designating it as present-mindedness. So engrossed am I in thinking about matters of importance that I often cannot remember routine trivia!

--I treasure the integrity of character that results from harmonizing what I feel with what I say and do. The basic respect that I have for myself comes from recognizing that my actions are not erratic, even though they lack full consistency. I have no desire to gain the whole world at the cost of my true self.

Love of Spouse

--Marital love has an in-spite-of as well as a because-of quality since it is unconditionally "for better, for worse." Thus I should not dwell on my wife's persistent shortcomings. Rather I should be gladdened by her redeeming qualities and be solicitous that her potentialities be brought to full flowering. Recognizing that all of us are to some degree the victims of childhood conditioning that cannot be altered, I should not expect that all undesirable traits will be changed.

--"To thine own self be true" is a maxim for goose and gander alike. I implore my wife to express sincerely her deepest convictions. I should be supportive of her efforts to become part of a community which, to use Paul's words, clothes itself with "compassion, kindness, humility, gentleness, and patience."[94]

Love of Self

--I love my capability of acting as a free individual. As a consequence of this I am outraged when I find that someone else has been exploiting me for ends that are alien to my own purposes. My individuality has been enhanced through the role flexibility that I enjoy. I receive monetary compensation for my performances as a teacher, departmental administrator, investment manager, and clergyman. But I also find gratifying my roles as a house husband, carpenter, painter, and mechanic.

Love of Spouse

--My relationship with my-wife must be an I-Thou one, for she is not an object to be manipulated. She should act from internal impulsion rather than from external compulsion. Marriage should promote individual distinction, not extinction. My spouse's uniqueness can be strengthened by encouraging her to express herself in a variety of paid or unpaid roles that engage her special talents.

A propos here are Kahlil Gibran's inspired words:

Fill each other's cup but drink not from one cup....
Sing and dance together and be joyous, but let each one of you be alone,
Even as the strings of a lute are alone though they quiver with the same music....
Stand together yet not too near together: for the pillars of the temple stand apart,
And the oak tree and the cypress grow not in each other's shadow.[95]

Conclusion

What can we make of the fact that a variety of intelligent people find in Paul diametrically opposing principles with respect to the status of women? A cynical response would be that historical sources are little more than a mirror for whatever ideology a person wishes to communicate. Hence, those who are convinced that Christianity should be in the vanguard of human liberation tend to

29

regard his letters as the first blast against monstrous sexism in Christian literature. On the other hand, those who are convinced that the church is a reactionary force vis à vis sexual equality see in Paul's letters a repressive patriarchy.

Ironically, the feminists who denounce Paul without qualification as one who was derogatory toward women show that they are unable to liberate themselves from traditional male interpreters. The truly independent feminist has, like Sarah Grimke, learned to use the historical and literary methods of modern critical scholarship in reading Paul's letters in full context. After removing male blinders she or he can become cognizant of the male chauvinist who sees no more than a reflection of his own image when he looks in the face of Paul. However, some appear to be so animated by prejudice against Paul that they prefer to attribute to him antifeminist developments of the post-apostolic church rather than look at his letters as sources to be exegeted intelligently. Bertrand Russell, for instance, regarded Paul's view of male-female relations as rather pathological. That philosopher held that it "can be regarded by sane people as a morbid aberration. The fact that it is embedded in Christian ethics has made Christianity throughout its whole history a force tending toward mental disorders and unwholesome views of life."[96]

A more balanced response would be to see Paul as a man in the process of being delivered by his Lord from the sexism that has been endemic to human cultures. Although he did not fully imitate Jesus' philogyny,[97] it is libelous to call him a misogynist. Indeed, he was more devoted to the feminine half of humanity than most men who have influenced Christianity. Feminists sensitive to historical context should find Paul more appealing than appalling. It has been demonstrated that Paul's appreciation of women was much greater than most of his translators and interpreters have wanted to admit. His writings, as well as the stories about him in the Acts of the Apostles,[98] reveal that he was a feminist who occasionally suffered a relapse. Paul's most grievous expression

30

of antifeminism was, as we have seen, in 1 Cor. 11:7, for it shows that he was not unbiased enough to appreciate the giant leap for humankind made by the author of the Genesis 1 creation account. On the other hand, the apostle's feminism is best expressed in Gal. 3:28, where he writes: "There is neither male nor female, for you are all one in Christ Jesus." How different this is from a common male thanksgiving of the world in which he lived! Both Jewish and Greek men expressed gratitude that they were not born female.[99] Mainline Christianity understandably chose to accept as normative Paul's androcentric statements because they comfortably fit into the prevailing milieu. Consequently, when the third century Montanists, on the basis of Gal. 3:28, permitted women to be leaders and priests, they were condemned as heretics.[100]

Paul's ambivalence toward women displays an attitude which is still much alive in the contemporary world. Looking back at him after many centuries of subsequent patriarchy, the suprising thing is not that he lacked full consistency but that he was able to extricate himself as much as he did from his cultural conditioning. He tried valiantly to follow Jesus, the reconciler, who had "broken down the dividing wall of hostility" between cultures and sexes in order to create "one new humanity in the place of two."[101]

NOTES

1. <u>Bernard</u> Shaw: <u>Complete Plays</u> (New York, 1962), Vol. V, p. 398.

2. Elizabeth Davis, <u>The First Sex</u> (Baltimore, 1972), p. 202.

3. G. B. Caird, "Paul and Women's Liberty," <u>Bulletin of John Ryland Library</u>, Vol. LIV, No. 2, Spring, 1972, p. 268.

4. Robin Scroggs, "Paul and the Eschatological Woman," <u>Journal of the American Academy of Religion</u>, Sept., 1972, p. 283.

5. Derwood Smith, "Paul and the Non-Eschatological Woman," <u>Ohio Journal of Religious Studies</u>, Mar., 1976, p. 18.

6. Tertullian, <u>On Monogamy</u> 3.

7. Jerome, <u>Against Jovinian</u> 1, 7.

8. Augustine, <u>Confessions</u> 2, 3.

9. Gunther Bornkamm, <u>Paul</u> (New York, 1971), p. 207; Rudolf Bultmann, <u>Theology of the New Testament</u> (New York, 1951), Vol. I, p. 202; Hans Conzelmann, <u>1 Corinthians</u> (Philadelphia, 1975), p. 115; <u>The Sayings of Jesus in the Churches of Paul</u> (Philadelphia, 1971), p. 84; J. S. Glen, <u>Pastoral Problems of First Corinthians</u> (London, 1965), p. 275; Joseph Klausner, <u>From Jesus to Paul</u> (Boston, 1943), p. 570; L. H. Marshall, <u>The Challenge of New Testament Ethics</u> (London, 1960), p. 336.

10. Johannes Weiss, <u>Earliest Christianity</u> (New York, 1937), Vol. II, p. 582.

11. Clarence Craig, "First Corinthians," <u>The Interpreter's Bible</u> (New York, 1953), Vol. X, p. 76.

12. E. g., William Barclay, <u>The Letters to the Corinthians</u> (Philadelphia, 1975), p. 58; Joachim Jeremias, <u>Abba</u> (Göttingen, 1966), p. 273; Philippe Menoud, "Mariage et célibat selon saint Paul," <u>Revue de Theologie et de Philosophie</u>, (1951), p. 26; John Ruef, <u>Paul's First Letter to Corinth</u> (Middlesex, 1971), p. 53.

13. David Smith, <u>Life and Letters of Paul</u> (London, 1920), p. 262.

14. E. W. Hunt, <u>Portrait of Paul</u> (London, 1968), p. 207.

15. 1 Cor. 7:1, 25; 8:1; 12:1; 16:1, 12.

16. 1 Cor. 6:12-13; 10:23.

17. See, e.g., the Revised Standard Version, New English Bible, and Today's English Version.

18. William Masters and Virginia Johnson, The Pleasure Bond (Boston, 1974), p. 11.

19. Geoffrey Chaucer, The Canterbury Tales, 11. 5739-5742.

20. Eleanor McLaughlin, "Equality of Souls, Inequality of Sexes" in Rosemary Ruether, ed. Religion and Sexism (New York, 1976), p. 225.

21. Cf. William Phipps, Was Jesus Married? (New York, 1970), pp. 82-89.

22. Wayne Meeks, "The Image of the Androgyne," History of Religions, Feb., 1974, p. 200.

23. Cf. 1 Cor. 12:3, 27.

24. Cf. Exodus 15:20; Judges 4:4; 2 Kings 22:14.

25. Cf. Acts 2:17-18; 21:9.

26. 1 Cor. 14:34. Although liberal scholars frequently attempt to eliminate the apparent contridiction between 1 Cor. 11:5 and this passage by arguing that Paul wrote only the former, there is little evidence to support treating 1 Cor. 14:34-36 as an interpolation by a later antifeminist. A number of scholars who see Paul as a feminist have resorted to literary surgery in order to defend their position. They often cut out from the Pauline corpus Ephesians and objectionable passages in 1 Corinthians. If they were to reduce the Pauline corpus exclusively to Galatians, then all problems of Paul's anti-feminism would be eliminated!

27. Cf. Ross Kraemer, Ecstatics and Ascetics: Studies in the Functions of Religious Activities for Women in the Greco-Roman World (Ann Arbor, 1976), pp. 117-132.

28. W. J. Burghardt, The Image of God in Man According to Cyril of Alexandria (Washington, 1957), p. 134.

29. Thomas Aquinas, Summa Theologica i, q. 94, 4; Augustine, On the Trinity 12, 7, 10.

33

30. Fernand Prat, The Theology of St. Paul (Westminster, Md., 1958), Vol. I, p. 121.

31. John Milton, Works (New York, 1931), Vol. IV, p. 76, 77.

32. John Milton, Paradise Lost, 4, 299.

33. Karl Barth, Church Dogmatics (Edinburgh, 1961), Vol. III/4, pp. 171-173.

34. David Laing, ed. The Works of John Knox (Edinburgh, 1855), Vol. IV, p. 386.

35. E. F. Scott, Paul's Epistle to the Romans (London, 1947), p. 79.

36. A. D. Nock, St. Paul (New York, 1963), p. 199.

37. The subscription in some ancient manuscripts at the end of this letter state that she carried the letter. Cf. William Sanday and Arthur Headlam, The Epistle to the Romans (New York, 1915), p. xxxvii.

38. Cf. Jean Danielou, The Ministry of Women in the Early Church (London, 1961), p. 14.

39. J. P. Migne, ed. Patrologia Graeca (Paris, 1857-1866), Vol. 14, col. 1278.

40. Pliny, Letters 10, 46.

41. 1 Clement 36:1; 61:3; 64.

42. E.g., 1 Chronicles 29:6; 2 Chronicles 8:10; 1 Esdras 2:12; 2 Maccabees 3:4.

43. E.g., 1 Thess. 5:12; 1 Tim. 3:5; 5:17; cf. Andre Dumas, "Biblical Anthropology and the Participation of Women in the Ministry of the Church" in Concerning the Ordination of Women (Geneva, 1964), p. 20.

44. Cf. Rom. 16:21; 2 Cor. 8:23; Philm. 24.

45. Phil. 4:2-3.

46. Acts 18:26; 28:23.

47. Ratified by Paul VI on Oct. 15, 1976, and published in The Pope Speaks 22 (Summer, 1977), p. 114.

48. Cf. C. H. Dodd, The Epistle of Paul to the Romans (London, 1932), pp. xxvi.

49. Acts 2:9; 18:2.

50. Gal. 2:7.

51. Cf. V. L. Bullough, The Subordinate Sex (Baltimore, 1974), p. 89.

52. Adolf Harnack, "Probabilia über die Adresse und den Verfasser des Hebräerbriefs," Zeitschrift für die neutestamentliche Wissenschaft (1900), Vol. I, pp. 16-41.

53. A. S. Peake, The Century Bible: Hebrews (London, n.d.), pp. 190-206.

54. L. A. Starr, The Bible Status of Woman (New York, 1926), pp. 190-206.

55. Rom. 16:7, Jerusalem Bible translation.

56. Cf. 1 Cor. 9:1; 15:7; Gal. 1:19.

57. Cf. J. A. Fitzmyer, "The Letter to the Romans," Jerome Biblical Commentary (Englewood Cliffs, N. J., 1968), Part 2, p. 330.

58. Chrysostom, Homilies on Romans 31.

59. Markus Barth, Ephesians 1-3 (Garden City, N. Y., 1974), pp. 36-50; A. Van Roon, The Authenticity of Ephesians (Leiden, 1974).

60. John Stuart and Harriet Taylor Mill, Essays on Sex Equality Chicago, 1970), p. 176.

61. Eph. 6:5; Col. 3:22; and Eph. 6:1; Col. 3:20.

62. Paul Bayne, An Entire Commentary upon the Whole Epistle of the Apostle Paul to the Ephesians (London, 1647), p. 640.

63. Simone De Beauvoir, The Second Sex (New York, 1968), p. 97.

64. Eugene Bianchi and Rosemary Ruether, From Machismo to Mutuality (New York, 1976), p. 135.

65. Marabel Morgan, The Total Woman (Old Tappan, N. J., 1973), p. 69, 80.

66. Judith M. Miles, The Feminine Principle (St. Louis, 1975), p. 44.

67. Milton, Paradise Lost, 4, 635-638.

68. Sarah Grimke, Letters on the Equality of the Sexes and the Condition of Woman (Boston, 1838), p. 90 (letter 13).

69. Masters and Johnson, op. cit., p. 257.

70. Song of Songs 2:16.

71. Mill, op. cit., p. 235.

72. Henry Bullinger, The Christian State of Matrimony 17.

35

73. J. H. Yoder, The Politics of Jesus (Grand Rapids, 1972), p. 181.

74. Mark 10:42-43, 45.

75. John 13:3-15; 15:15.

76. Phil. 2:3-8.

77. Eph. 4:32.

78. Eph. 5:2.

79. Markus Barth, The Broken Wall (Chicago, 1959), p. 233.

80. Rom. 13:9; Mark 12:31.

81. Luke 10:25-37.

82. Augustine, On Christian Doctrine 1, 24-26.

83. Aristotle, Nicomachean Ethics 1168b.

84. Erich Fromm, The Art of Loving (New York, 1956), pp. 48-54.

85. Eph. 5:29.

86. Eph. 5:28.

87. Song of Songs 7:1-10.

88. Eph. 4:26.

89. Eph. 4:31.

90. Col. 3:18.

91. Cf. 2 Cor. 5:17-20.

92. Rom. 12:3.

93. Eph. 4:15.

94. Col. 3:12.

95. Kahlil Gibran, The Prophet (New York, 1927), p. 17.

96. Bertrand Russell, Marriage and Morals (New York, 1929), p. 48.

97. Cf. William Phipps, The Sexuality of Jesus (New York, 1973), pp. 53-76.

98. Acts 16:13-18; 17:4.

99. Tosephta Berekhoth 7, 18; Diogenes Laertius, Lives of the Philosophers 2, 33.

100. Cf. Epiphanius, Against Heresies 49.

101. Eph. 2:14-15.

CHAPTER 2

JEROME'S MANHANDLING OF SCRIPTURE

For more than a thousand years Jerome has been regarded as
the most authoritative post-apostolic interpreter of the Bible who
lived during the early centuries of Christianity. In the Middle
Ages he was widely hailed as "Doctor Maximus sacris Scripturis
explanandis."[1] Jerome continues to be held in high esteem by
some Protestant and Roman Catholic scholars. Robert Grant, for
example, writing in The Interpreter's Bible, calls Jerome "the
greatest exegete of the ancient church."[2] Likewise, the editors
of The Jerome Bible Commentary refer to Jerome as "the foremost
Scripture scholar among the Church Fathers, a pioneer in biblical
criticism."[3]

The reputation of Jerome was established by his literary
skills and by his monastic lifestyle. He was the most learned
scholar of his day and the last ancient classicist of merit,
having rare ability in Greek and Hebrew as well as in Latin.
Jerome's knowledge of Hebrew resulted from a self-imposed penance.
He believed that a study of that difficult language, virtually
unknown to Latin scholars, might pommel his sex drive. He recalls:
"In my youth, when the desert walled me in with its solitude, I
was still unable to endure the promptings of sin and the natural
heat of my blood. Although I tried by frequent fasts to break the
force of both, my mind still surged with evil thoughts. To subdue its turbulence I asked a monk who was a converted Jew to teach
me Hebrew."[4] Jerome goes on to testify that the study was grueling
but it bore "sweet fruit." By the turn of the fifth century he
was able to translate the Bible from its original languages into
the Latin Vulgate. For the next millennium that version was
quoted as the decisive authority throughout European Christianity.
Moreover, during that time most churchmen accepted without question
Jerome's biblical interpretations as well as his translations.

37

Jerome lived during a time when the ancient Roman empire was tottering and when many Christians were attracted by ascetics who advocated withdrawing from the decaying urban life and into monastic communities. The time was ripe for the letters, diatribes, commentaries, and sermons of Jerome which had abstinence as their central theme. In introducing his writings, W. H. Fremantle comments: "His general attitude is that which disdained the common joys of life, which thought of eating, drinking, clothing, or lodging, and most of all marriage, as physical indulgences which should be suppressed as far as possible."[5]

Jerome was able to spread his outlook into the Eastern Mediterranean by making Bethlehem his base of operations during the latter part of his life. It appears that he had agreed to leave Rome because of a scandal resulting from his close friendship with a wealthy widow named Paula.[6] She was soon to join him in Palestine and become his companion and patron until her death two decades later.

The positions that Jerome expressed were especially valued because most Christians accepted him for what he claimed to be--a champion of orthodoxy. "From my very cradle," he affirms, "I have been nurtured on Catholic milk; and no one can be a better churchman than one who has never been a heretic."[7] Pope Damasus, who commissioned Jerome to make a new Latin version of Scriptures, probably supported the common opinion that Jerome deserved to become the next supreme pontiff. Regarding the popularity which he once had in Rome, he brags: "Almost everyone concurred in judging me worthy of the highest office in the church. My words were always of the lips of Damasus, of blessed memory. Men called me saintly, humble, and eloquent."[8] However, Jerome was never given any high position in the church.

The invectiveness which permeates most of Jerome's writings may have been due, in part, to his resentment over not being selected as Bishop of Rome. Also, his celibate discipline caused him to be scornful of those who enjoyed life's pleasures. In his perceptive biography, Frederic Farrar writes: "Jerome, who had become a monk to subdue the passions of the flesh, does not seem to think it any harm to indulge himself to any extent in the passions of the mind....In all his polemics he gives full reins to envy, hatred, malice, and all uncharitableness."[9]

Jerome's wrath was especially directed toward a monk named Jovinian who magnanimously claimed that the Bible does not exalt to a higher status the celibate life. Jovinian's writings have unfortunately not survived but it is possible to recover some of his position in the writings of Jerome, even though that adversary judged them to be "nauseating trash"[10] and presents only what he considered to be Jovinian's most objectionable views. Jovinian had said to consecrated virgins: "You have chosen a life of chastity on account of the present distress. You determined on the course in order to be holy in body and spirit. Do not be proud: you and your married sisters are members of the same church."[11] Jerome writes: "The question at issue between myself and Jovinian is that he puts marrige on a level with virginity, while I make it inferior....He has been condemned because he has dared to set matrimony on an equality with perpetual chastity."[12] Jovinian had been excommunicated and his position had been condemned by Pope Siricius and Bishop Ambrose before Jerome added his condemnation.[13]

How did Jovinian support his controversial view that the virginal life and the married life were regarded equally virtuous by the Bible writers? Regarding the flood story, he states: "Only Noah, his wife, and his sons and their wives were saved at the deluge, although there must have been in the world many persons not of marriageable age, and therefore presumably virgins."[14] He argues that virtually all of the patriarchs, prophets, and monarchs of Israel were married and that most of the apostles participated in that holy estate. To show that most of the apostles were married Jovinian quoted Paul's query: "Do we not have the right to be accompanied by a wife as the other apostles and the brothers of the Lord, and Cephas?"[15] Jesus' citation from the Eden story about man and woman being joined into "one flesh" and his participation in the marriage festivities at Cana are presented by Jovinian as evidence that the married state is no less excellent than the single state.[16] He also notes that the New Testament sanctions married bishops who have children in their households.[17] These interpretations of Jovinian are deemed sound by biblical scholars today.

The treatment that follows shows that Jerome, in spite of his linguistic genius, was unfaithful to the general biblical outlook on marital intercourse. In historical sequence his invalid Old and New Testament interpretations will be sampled. Although they are worthless as biblical exposition, they afford fascinating insights into the mind of one of the foremost ascetics of the Christian church and into a sexual outlook that was dominant for at least half of the entire history of Christianity.

Jerome, through eisegesis, finds virginity advocated from the first pages of Scripture onward. He notices that God's declaration of the goodness of the created acts was omitted only on the second day of the creation week. Since the number two signified marriage for Jerome, he concludes that the opening chapter of Genesis suggests that marriage is not good.[18] He conveniently overlooks in that chapter the climax of creation when, on the "very good" sixth day, God's first blessing is pronounced on sexual expression. In Genesis 2 Jerome finds the requirement of fasting established, for Adam was commanded to abstain from the fruit of one tree in the Garden of Eden. Jerome associated this with his notion that certain foods were sexual stimulants.[19] Hence, it was only after the first couple tasted of the presumed aphrodisiac fruit that they succumbed to temptation and reaped its horrific consequences. "As regards Adam and Eve," Jerome writes, "we must maintain that before the fall they were virgins in paradise: but after they sinned and were cast out of paradise they were immediately married."[20] Thus, "virginity is natural while wedlock only follows guilt."[21] Jerome believed that Adam was not as much to blame as his wife (even though each knew about

40

the forbidden fruit and voluntarily violated the divine prohibition).
"Always bear in mind that it was a woman who expelled the tiller
of paradise from his heritage," Jerome asserts.[22]

It is Jerome's conviction that married women tend to emulate
Eve, the tempter. Thus, for example, Job's wife is portrayed as
the devil's advocate. After stripping Job of his wealth, children,
and health, the devil's most bitter scrouge of all is poured out.
Jerome states: "The devil left him nothing but his tongue and his
wife: the former for blaspheming and the latter for tempting.
The devil had not forgotten that old craftiness by which he deceived
Adam through a woman; therefore, he attacks Job through his wife,
reckoning that he can always deceive man through woman."[23]

Jerome admits that the Pentateuch personalities were married,
but, on discovering that there is no mention of wife or child for
Joshua, he concludes that the leader of the Palestinian crusade
was a lifelong virgin. This illogic rivals that of Jerome's
contemporary Pelagius who allegedly claimed that Abel was sinless
because the Bible does not explicitly state of him, as it does for
the humans previous to him, that he sinned.[24] Jerome goes on to
assert that God honored celibate Joshua more than married Moses
by permitting the former to live in the Promised Land before his
death.[25] But Moses should be given credit, Jerome thought, for
establishing the "holy man" ideal. The exhortation in Leviticus,
"You shall be holy," is taken by Jerome to be a plea for the
monastic life, even though marriage was required of the levitical
priests.[26]

By converting an indulgence into a prohibition Jerome also
found support for sexual asceticism elsewhere in the Mosaic law.
According to Deuteronomy, a newly wed man was given a one year
deferment from military service so that he could go home and
"rejoice with his wife."[27] Jerome, however, twists this endorse-
ment of the pleasurableness of marital sexuality into a requirement for celibate warriors. He claims: "He who has married a
wife...is forbidden to go to battle. For he who is the slave of

his wife cannot be the Lord's soldier."[28]

Jerome presumes that he can proclaim on the authority of Moses not only that it is holier to be unwed but that a woman, whether virginal or not, is a cultic pollution hazard. Going beyond the Genesis story, which does not contain a "curse" on woman, he believes that menstruation is a sign that Eve and her daughters have been "cursed by God."[29] "Nothing is so unclean as a woman in her periods," Jerome writes.[30] Probably due to his influence a canon law was enacted in his time which banned women from the eucharistic altar. That law still remains operative in Roman Catholicism and is an unpublicized basis for reserving the offices of acolyte and priest for males.[31]

The ingenuity of Jerome is well displayed in his treatment of David and Solomon and the poetry that they were reputed to have written. Jerome is able to find in those much married monarchs arguments for the virginal life. David's intimacies with women, including sleeping with maiden Abishag in his old age, is explained in one of Jerome's writings as a result of the Israelite living before the Gospel era.[32] Yet, in another writing about the same time, Jerome rejects the literal account of Abishag warming David's body. Rather, she represents wisdom which increases as the body decays. Hence the meaning of David's snuggling is this: "Let wisdom alone embrace me; let Abishag, who grows not old, nestle in my bosom. She is undefiled and a virgin forever; for although she daily conceives and unceasingly brings to birth, like Mary she is stainless."[33]

Verses from David's psalms are also interpreted by Jerome from the stance of sexual abstinence. He found problematic a reference in Psalm 128:3 to a wife being a blessing from God. In some of his writings Jerome attempts to explain away this honoring of matrimony by maintaining that the psalm expresses an outlook of ancient Judaism that has been rejected by Christianity.[34] However, in one sermon he exhorts his congregation to interpret the "wife" as an allegorical reference to wisdom. Just as Solomon was personifying wisdom when he said, "She will honor you if you embrace her," so David was claiming that God would bless virgins with the growth of wisdom.[35]

Another psalm contains this savage cry for revenge against Judah's Babylonian captors: "Happy shall be he who seizes and smashes your little ones against the rock." Presuming that "little ones" is an oblique reference to little lusts, Jerome confesses: "I saw a woman, for instance; I was filled with desire for her. If I do not at once cut off that sinful desire and take hold of it, as it were, by the foot and dash it against a rock until sensual passion abates, it will be too late afterwards when the smoldering fire has burst into flame. Happy the man who puts the knife instantly to sinful passion and smashes it against a rock! Now the Rock is Christ."[36]

The Psalter concludes with a call to dance and praise God with many musical instruments, one of which is the tambourine. Jerome states: "A tambourine is not made of flesh but of skin, and as long as we are carnal, we are not tambourines. You cannot make a tambourine unless you remove all the flesh and draw the skin tight; a tambourine cannot contract; the membrane must be stretched taut." The cryptic moral found here is expressed in this exhortation: "Let us crucify our bodies for Christ and sing to God with a tambourine of this kind."[37]

The pièce de résistance in Jerome's counterattack against Jovinian is Solomon's Song of Songs. There is no portion of the Bible of similar length that Jerome alluded to more frequently in his effort to vindicate virginity. The purpose of the Song can best be understood, Jerome contended, by placing the book at the end of a sequence of books which the monarch wrote. In Ecclesiastes Solomon reflects on his multiple marriages and admits that, among the hundreds of women that he knew, he has been unable to find one who is upright.[38] That wisest of kings looked forward, according to Jerome, to the Gospel dispensation when those who had been under the law could "refrain from embracing."[39] Then "the forests

of marriage" will be "cut down by the chastity of the Gospel."[40]
In Proverbs, Solomon refers to an infertile wife's longing for
children in this way: "Three things are never satisfied; four
never say, 'Enough': Sheol, the barren womb, the earth ever
thirsty for water, and the fire which never says, 'Enough.'"[41]
Jerome, presuming that Solomon was commenting on the sexual desire
of all women, writes: "Woman's love in general is accused of ever
being insatiable; put it out, it bursts into flame; give it plenty,
it is again in need; it enervates a man's mind, and engrosses all
thought except for the passion which it feeds."[42]

Jerome's own neurosis is mirrored in his characterization of
the opposite sex. "When I was living in the desert," he confesses,
"how often did I fancy myself among the pleasures of Rome!...I
often found myself in the midst of dancing girls. My face was
pale and my frame chilled with fasting; yet my mind was burning
with desire and the fires of lust kept bubbling up."[43] Jerome's
imagination of Roman entertainment was derived from his firsthand
experience. "I extol virginity to the skies," he says, "not
because I myself possess it, but because, not possessing it, I
admire it all the more."[44] Because Jerome presumes that Solomon's
sexual experiences were somewhat parallel to his own, he writes:
"No one can know better than he who has suffered through them,
what a wife or woman is."[45]

According to Jerome, the Song of Songs is penitent Solomon's
ode to unsullied virginity.[46] How could Jerome interpret the Song
as a paean to perpetual virginity when the book seems to be focused
on physical lovemaking? He was much influenced by the self-
castrated Origen who had maintained that the true significance of
the Song is altogether different from its apparent meaning. Jerome
regarded Origen's sermons on the Song as the finest writing of that
scholar and so Jerome translated them into Latin.[47] Origen had
exhorted Christians to mortify the flesh before approaching the
Song, for the book has nothing to do with human lovers.[48] Jerome
followed his mentor in detesting the actual practice of coitus

while being engrossed in it on a fantasy level.

In Jerome's allegorical interpretation of the Song of Songs, the bride is the Christian woman who has vowed than her hymen will never be penetrated. The groom poetically alludes to this unruptured condition when he praises his bride as "a garden locked, a fountain sealed."[49] That consecrated virgin is given instructions in the Song on how to protect her virtue. She should not go out in public and she should beware of receiving guests in her home. When a man seeking physical marriage knocks she should answer with one of these verses from the Song: "I am a wall and my breasts are its towers," or "I have washed my feet: how can I defile them?"[50] The Song also warns against the active girl who rejects the cloistered life. Her brazen determination and its tragic outcome is expressed in these lines: "I will rise now and go about the streets....I will seek him whom my soul loves....I sought him, but found him not....The watchmen found me as they patrolled the city; they beat me, they wounded me, they took away my veil."[51] The moral of this is that "Jesus is jealous and does not wish that others see your face."[52] As in the Gospel parable of the wise and foolish virgins, bridegroom Jesus passes by those who have not been awaiting his coming. When Jesus approaches the wise virgin, she will exclaim, "Hark! My beloved is knocking, saying, 'Open to me, my sister, my love.'"[53]

It is seen that Jerome finds in the Song of Songs words of Jesus, "the author and prince of virginity." He boldly says of himself, "I am the rose of Sharon and the lily of the valleys."[54] The purpose of this exquisite flower is stated thus: "When Jesus was crowned with thorns and bore our sins and suffered for us, it was to make the roses of virginity and the lilies of chastity grow."[55] His crucifixion is allegedly prefigured in this line from the Song, "My beloved is white and ruddy."[56] Understood spiritually, "white" and "ruddy" refer to unsoiled and bloody martrydom respectively.[57]

The graphically depicted consummation of the bride and groom in the Song of Songs is transposed by Jerome. Jesus calls: "Arise, my love, my fair one, and come away."[58] To the spotless virgin he will say, "You are wholly beautiful, my love; there is no blemish in you."[59] Drawing on imagery from the Song, Jerome counsels the virgins, "Ever let the Bridegroom fondle....He will put his hand through the opening and will caress your body. You will arise trembling and cry, 'I am lovesick.'"[60] In reflecting on this abiding ecstasy the bride says, "Many waters cannot quench love, neither can floods drown it."[61]

Jerome also encouraged virginal men to identify with the bride and, in effect, have a simulated homosexual liaison with Jesus. The Song of Songs encourages lovers to drink deeply of wine, and this means that both young men and women should become intoxicated with virginity.[62] Jerome alludes to the sensual Song in advising a scholarly monk: "Let the divine love carry you out of yourself; and then seek upon your bed him whom your soul loves, and boldly say: 'I sleep, but my heart is awake.' When you have found him and have taken hold of him, let him not go....Give to him your breasts; let him suck your learned bosom."[63]

Largely due to Jerome's infusion into Latin Christianity of allegorical interpretations of the Song of Songs, it became "the book which was most read and most frequently commented on in the medieval cloister."[64] Allegorists who find in the Song a discarnate mysticism binding God and believer have abounded until recent times. They have had such a heavy impact on the church that even today most Christians do not realize that the Song says nothing explicitly about God and much about connubial passion. Many contemporaries have yet to appreciate a judgment made about Jerome's interpretation of Jewish Scriptures by Farrar. A century ago he wrote: "Except in fantastic perversions of the Song of Songs, which tells when rightly understood in the very opposite direction, there is not one syllable in the whole Old Testament which sanctions that exaltation of virginity which was a fundamental article of monkish morals."[65]

The prophetic books were, for Jerome, sources of pronouncements of sexual abstinence and forecasts of the era of virginity that will characterize the Christian dispensation. Ezekiel was viewed as one whose religious commitment improved after being deprived of marital intercourse. That prophet reports: "My wife died in the evening and on the next morning I did as I was commanded."[66] According to Jerome, the death of Ezekiel's spouse gave the prophet fuller liberty to devote himself to spiritual concerns.[67] In other prophecies Jerome found allusions to the virginal conception of Jesus. Hosea proclaims: "The wind of the Lord shall come up from the wilderness and his fountain shall dry up."[68] Jerome states: "When it is said that 'he shall come up from the wilderness,' the Virgin's womb is indicated, which without sexual intercourse or impregnation has given to us God in the form of an infant who is able to dry...the fountain of lust."[69] A similar interpretation is given to this oracle of Jeremiah: "The Lord has created a new thing on the earth; a woman protects a man."[70] Jerome found hidden there a prophecy of Mary's miraculous conception by which "the Father of all things is contained in a virgin's womb."[71] Again, Daniel foretelling "a stone cut out of a mountain without hands" signified for Jerome that Jesus would be conceived of a virgin without sexual intercourse.[72]

As might be expected, Jerome's sexual prejudices can be detected in his translations as well as in his interpretations. For example, in the Vulgate, Tobit 6:18 is given an expansion of the original text that "comes out of Jerome's head rather than out of any manuscript."[73] Accordingly, he has Raphael instructing Tobias to engage in a three night sexual fast before consummating his wedding. The angel sanctions, after that period of continence, coitus which from a desire for procreation rather than from erotic passion. Also, in Tobit 8:6 Jerome omits a quotation from Gen. 2:18, probably because it does not support his view that reproduction is the purpose of marriage, and in Tobit 8:9 he has Tobias

47

vowing to God that he has married "only for the love of posterity."
These interpretive alterations do violence to the context of this
book of the Apocrypha. As J. C. Dancy points out, the Tobit tale
teaches that "sex is good but married love is better."[74] Jerome's
biases were presumed to be Holy Scripture in the medieval era, so
the clergy counselled newly weds to let their sexual desires cool
for several days before engaging in intercourse.[75]

Jerome believed that sexual renunciation was the main theme
of the Gospel and that its pivotal personalities practiced what
they preached. Forerunner John the Baptist must have been a virgin,
Jerome reasoned, because Luke states that he was "in the spirit
and power of Elijah."[76] But how was Jerome sure that Elijah, whom
Jovinian had included in a list of married persons, was a virgin?
Jerome's certainty rests of the "gird his loins" expression used
of Elijah.[77] That frequently used biblical idiom refers to pre-
paring for rigorous activity, and is roughly equivalent to what
"tighten your belt" or "roll up your sleeves" is for those wearing
modern clothing. However, for Jerome the expression pertains not
to adjusting one's robe but to repressing one's below-the-belt urges.
Job's description of the devil, Jerome contends, demonstrates that
"loins" is a euphemism for "genitals."[78] Job calls the devil
Behemoth and asserts that "his strength is in his loins."[79] It
is commonly recognized, Jerome continues, that the devil uses the
genitals as his springboard for attack. Hence, to say that a man
"gird his loins" was, for Jerome, a circumlocution for saying that
he "confined and mortified" his penis.[80] It was necessary for John
to keep his penis deadened "so that by a virgin prophet the virgin
Lord might be both announced and baptized."[81] Jerome's tortured
exegesis was effective, for even now most Christians have no doubt
that John was a celibate.

In Jerome's time the virginal ideal was called into question
by those who believed that the mother and the apostles of Jesus
did not devote themselves to perpetual virginity. Helvidius held
that the states of virginity and marriage were of equal glory

48

because Mary was a virgin before Jesus was born and a partici-
pant in marital sexuality afterwards.[82] Evidence for her
latter situation rested, in part, on Matthew's claim that
Joseph "knew her not until she had borne a son."[83] Jerome, in
addressing Helvidius, has more than his customary contempt for
those with opinions differing form his own. "You most ignorant of
men," he exclaims, "by disregarding the whole field of Scripture
you have brought disgrace upon the Virgin with your madness."[84]
Jerome then dismisses Helvidius' sensible interpretation of
Matthew's nativity account by arguing that the verb "know" does
not there refer to carnal knowledge. "Know" often refers to
factual knowledge in the Bible, as in this statement: "The boy
Jesus stayed behind in Jerusalem and his parents knew it not."[85]
Therefore, Jerome presumed that Matthew meant that Joseph's understanding of Mary's miraculous conception did not fully flower
until she gave birth to Jesus. It would have been unconscionable,
Jerome maintained, for Joseph to have "dared to touch the temple
of God, the abode of the Holy Spirit, the mother of his Lord."[86]

Helvidius also used as proof of his position the reference in
the Gospels to several "brothers" of Jesus, the "first-born son"
of Mary.[87] Jerome's rebuttal is to point out that "every only
child is a first-born child" and that "brother" in Scripture may
refer to a cousin who is not a uterine relation.[88] Jerome thinks
that the "brothers" of Jesus are the sons of the sister of Jesus'
mother, Mary the wife of Clopas.[89] Hence, both Joseph and his
wife are claimed by Jerome to have been perpetual virgins.[90]

Jerome believed that the mother of Jesus was not only a virgin
before and after her singular giving of birth, but that her hymen
was not broken during that parturition. In spite of the fact that
Luke referred to Jesus as one who "opened the womb," Jerome held
that there was a miraculous delivery which enabled Mary to remain
"a fountain sealed."[91] In Jerome's mind, Jesus' passing through
Mary's closed vulva is parallel to his passing through a closed

49

door after his resurrection.[92] This docetic doctrine of Jerome, which denies to Jesus a full participation in human birth, became accepted as Catholic dogma. It is interesting to note that not even credulous Jerome accepted this fantastic outlook in his earlier writings.[93]

Jesus' aim during his days in the flesh was to live the paradisal life of virginity and to enable holy men and to enable holy men and women to "manifest themselves even in this life as angels."[94] That was the meaning which Jerome wrested from Jesus' assertion that there is no marriage institution in the resurrected life and that those who attain it "are like angels in heaven."[95] Jerome, presuming angels to be sexless, implored earthly virgins to remain sexually inactive in order to get a headstart on the heavenly life.[96] By austerities they can quench the flame of passion "and while in the body live as though out of it."[97] The reward at judgment day for this stupendous effort will make it worthwhile. Jerome applied to the life after death the conclusion one of Jesus' parables which states that the good soil brought forth "a hundred-fold, some sixty, some thirty."[98] The yields represent, from greatest to least, consecrated virgins, chaste widows, and pious spouses. What suggests that the lowest yield pertains to matrimony? Jerome's quaint response was that the Roman numeral XXX symbolizes the kissing and interlocking of husband and wife![99] He compares the value of virginity to gold and condones marriage because it is the goose that lays the golden egg. From coitus comes virgins; from thorns, roses; from shells, pearls.[100] Jesus did not completely devalue marriage because there is a need for a "seed plot out of which virginity springs."[101] However, even in the passage where this partial approval of marriage is given, Jerome loses all his equilibrium and declares on the highest authority that marriage is not a good at all. The Gospels, he points out, contain this lament for mothers who will suffer during the conflicts at the end of the age: "Alas for those who are pregnant and for those who nurse in those days!"[103]

Given Jerome's low esteem of marriage, it is understandable that he was embarrassed that the patron saint of his Roman Church had married. If Peter had known better, Jerome contended, he would never have married, but he took a wife before he met Jesus. As soon as Peter became a disciple he cast aside his fish net and his wife.[104] Accordingly, after Jesus advised a rich man to dispose of his goods, Peter spoke on behalf of the disciples: "Lo, we have left everything and followed you."[105] That statement showed Jerome that any would-be follower who is espoused ought to abandon his wife on responding to Jesus' call.[106]

John was Jerome's favorite apostle because he believed that John was a lifelong virgin. Jovinian's contention that John had married was dismissed by Jerome, who accepted the story in the apocryphal Acts of John that the apostle walked out on his own marriage feast to follow Jesus.[107] Also, Jerome believed that the Gospel allegedly written by that apostle contains a two-fold testimony to the virginity of its author. First, it was because of John's virginal state that he could truthfully assert at the Last Supper that "he was more beloved by our Lord and [could] lay upon the breast of Jesus." Second, at the crucifixion "the virgin mother was entrusted by the virgin Lord to the virgin disciple." John's virginity gave him the prophetic insight to write the book of Revelation as well as the Fourth Gospel. Thus, in Jerome's estimation, John was more virtuous than Peter and it was only out of deference to age that John was not made head of the church. This comparison is given by Jerome: "Peter is an apostle and John is an apostle: the married man and the virgin. But Peter is only an apostle: John is an apostle, an evangelist, and a prophet.... Virginity explained what marriage could not know."[108]

Jerome defended his criticism of matrimony by claiming that he was "much more gentle toward married persons than Paul was disposed to be."[109] Several verses in various letters of Paul and one chapter of one of his letters to Corinthian Christians provided Jerome with much of his ascetic ammunition. He presumed that Paul

51

was referring to marital sexuality when he denounced those who live "in the flesh." Paul wrote: "He who sows to his own flesh will from the flesh reap corruption."[110] This is interpreted by Jerome to mean that a husband is corrupt if he lacks continence and plants sperms in his wife.[111] Again, Paul stated: "Those who are in the flesh cannot please God."[112] On this Jerome comments: "They who perform the functions of marriage love the wisdom of the flesh, and therefore are in the flesh."[113] The higher way is to heed Paul's admonition to present one's body a living sacrifice unto God. Jerome thought that the apostle was advocating celibacy that would "consecrate to eternal chastity a living offering acceptable to God and free from all stain."[114] Actually, Paul did not closely associate "in the flesh" with sexual indulgence. The phrase refers to those qualities that block the expression of "love, joy, peace, patience, kindness, goodness, faithfulness, gentleness, and self-control."[115] Where can these fruits of the Spirit better be nurtured to maturity than in the intimate life of the family?

So obsessed was Jerome with sex that he also wrongly identifies "flesh" with sexual desire in another Pauline context. He was the first to suggest that Paul was referring to a struggle against sexual temptation when he told of "a thorn in the flesh" which harassed him.[116] That interpretation became popular among celibates even though there is no contextual support for it.[117] Perhaps Jerome found it sexually disturbing even to hear a woman singing hymns, because, allegedly on Paul's authority, Jerome permitted only males to engage in congregational singing.[118]

It was Paul's discussion of marriage in 1 Corinthians 7 that Jerome most admired. He believed that it exalted priestly celibacy for men and consecrated virginity for women. Jerome noted that Paul permitted coital abstinence during a period of prayer,[119] and that he instructed his followers in another letter to "pray always."[120] "If we are to pray always," Jerome argued, "it follows that we must never be in the bondage of wedlock, for as often as I render my wife her due I cannot pray."[121] Jerome comments: "A priest must always pray, so he must be released from the duties of marriage." The clerical vocation should not be forbidden to the man who has married, but he should be sexually continent after ordination. Indeed, "a man who generates children by his wife after becoming a bishop should be condemned as an adulterer."[122]

Acknowledging that he was single at the time of writing, Paul asserts, "I wish that all were as I am."[123] According to Jerome, this is what Paul meant: "I desire that you be imitators of me as I also am of Christ, who was a Virgin born of a Virgin, uncorrupt of her who was uncorrupt. We, because we are men, cannot imitate our Lord's nativity; but we may at least imitate his life."[124] Jerome was either unaware of, or did not want to admit that the letters of Paul make no mention of the alleged virginal conception or celibate life of Jesus.

Paul's assurance that it is not sinful for a virgin to marry[125] made Jerome uneasy. He believed that the apostle did not have in mind those who had dedicated themselves to lifelong virginity. Regarding the latter Jerome says: "Should one of these marry, she will have damnation."[126] He thought that the Lord inspired Paul to write that "the unmarried woman or virgin is anxious about the affairs of the Lord, how to be holy in body and spirit, but the married woman is anxious about worldly affairs, how to please her husband."[127] That simplistic contrast is further accentuated by Jerome: "The virgin's aim is to appear less lovely; she will debase herself so as to hide her natural attractions. The married woman paints herself before the mirror, and, to the insult of her Maker, strives to improve on her natural beauty...Tell me, I ask you, where amid all this is there any opportunity to think of God?"[128]

In spite of the venerated stature that Jerome has long had, he was devoted more to the imposition of his sexual asceticism on to Scripture than to the exposition of the views of the biblical writers. The headwaters of that asceticism were pagan, and this fact is displayed in Jerome's review of Greco-Roman ascetic history. To prove that virginity was given prominence in non-biblical religions, he calls attention to the high status held by the Roman Vestal Virgins. He refers to the cults of the virgin goddesses Minerva and Diana, as well as to the virginal conception legends of Plato, Buddha, and the founders of the city of Rome. Jerome concludes his lengthy treatment of pagan celibacy by telling of the eunuch priests of Athens.[129] In his attack on marriage he adduces some of the misogynistic arguments of Aristotle, Theophrastus, Seneca, Juvenal, and Porphyry. In this regard David Wiesen shows that "Jerome recast the popular philosophy of paganism into a vehicle of Christian propaganda."[130] Jerome was not only heavily influenced by Hellenistic morality but also by the rapidly spreading Manicheanism from the Middle East which prohibited indulgence in wine, meat, and sex.

Attention has been especially directed in this study to those passages where Jerome's biblical interpretations were distinctively different from the mainstream of early Christianity. Examination of those passages reinforces a concluding evaluation by John Kelly in his recent excellent biography of Jerome. Kelly writes: "At the heart of his teaching lay the conviction that chastity was the quintessence of the gospel message, and that its supreme exemplification and proof was Mary, the virgin mother of the virgin Saviour."[131] Jerome did more than any other person to make the perpetual virginity of Mary an intrinsic part of Catholic orthodoxy and to exalt celibacy as the only acceptable lifestyle for those in religious vocations.

Jerome's distortions of the original Judeo-Christian sexual ethic also sheds light on the acid stream of misogyny which has polluted church tradition. As I have demonstrated in earlier writings, the founder of Christianity was a philogynist.[132] To inculcate Jesus' radically different outlook on women demanded more courage than the pedestrian churchmen could muster. Consequently the sexual standards of the gentile church generally reflected the dominant mores of Greco-Roman culture. Hence, within a few centuries, pristine purity for a woman was inseparable from virginity. Jerome admired only those women who were sexually inactive, since "omni coitus impurus."[133] Thus, he considered the widow who remarries to be as disgusting as a dog that returns to its own vomit.[134] Among sexually inactive women he admired the virgin the most because in her "even the distinction of sex is lost."[135] According to Jerome she exemplifies what the human creation was like before sin and what it will be like after redemption. On the other hand, it is those sexually active women living between the "fall of man" and the judgment day who are responsible for much of the ills of humanity.

As a self-appointed apostle of virginity Jerome was guilty of clever but crass manhandling of Scripture. Had he not been so fanatically devoted to his mission, his non-sequitur tirades and witty satires would be more amusing. Far from establishing sound principles for biblical interpretation, Jerome's perverse treatments lend credence to the old saw of cynics that anything can be proved by shrewd students of Scripture.

It is fitting retribution to give Chaucer's Wife of Bath the last word here. The pleasures of one of her husbands included beating her and reading Against Jovinian. The wife, realizing that the stories she knew were tales told by clerics and noticing that Jerome only spoke well of sexually abstinent women, muses how different history would read if it had been woman-handled. Here is her pert protest:

By God, if wommen hadde writen stories,
As clerkes han with-inne hir oratories,
They wolde han writen of men more wikkednesse
Than all the mark of Adam may redresse.[136]

NOTES

1. Cf. Francis Murphy, ed. A Monument to Saint Jerome (New York, 1952), pp. 37, 68; The Letters of Abelard and Heloise (New York, 1926), p. 259.

2. Robert M. Grant, "History of the Interpretation of the Bible," The Interpreter's Bible (New York, 1952), I, p. iii.

3. The Jerome Biblical Commentary (Englewood Cliffs, N. J., 1968), p. xx.

4. Jerome, Letters 125, 12.

5. W. H. Fremantle, "The Principal Works of St. Jerome," The Nicene and Post-Nicene Fathers (Grand Rapids, 1954), Second Series, VI, p. xxx.

6. Cf. John N. Kelly, Jerome (London, 1975), pp. 113-114.

7. Jerome, Letters 82, 2.

8. Ibid., 45, 3.

9. Frederic W. Farrar, Lives of the Fathers (Edinburgh, 1889), II, p. 272.

10. Jerome, Against Jovinian 1, 4. Hereafter cited as AJ.

11. AJ 1, 5.

12. Jerome, Letters 48, 2.

13. Siricius, Letters 7; Ambrose, Letters 42, 14.

14. AJ 1, 5.

15. AJ 1, 16-26; 1 Cor. 9:5.

16. AJ 1, 5 and 40.

17. AJ 1, 34; 1 Tim. 3:2, 4; Titus 1:6.

18. AJ 1, 16.

19. AJ 2, 7 and 15.

20. AJ 1, 16.

21. Jerome, Letters 22, 19.

22. Ibid., 52, 5.

23. Jerome, Homilies 73.

24. Augustine, Letters 179, 8.

25. AJ 1, 22.

26. Jerome, Letters 118, 5; Lev. 19:2; 21:13.

27. Deut. 20:7; 24:5.

28. AJ 1, 20.

29. Jerome, Against Helvidius 20. Hereafter cited as AH.

30. Jerome, Commentary on Zechariah, Migne, ed. Patrologia Latina 25, col 1517.

31. Synod of Laodicea, canon 44; cf. Rosemary Ruether ed. Religion and Sexism (New York, 1976), p. 273.

32. AJ 1, 24.

33. Jerome, Letters 52, 2-4.

34. AJ 1, 22; Jerome, Letters 22, 21; 123, 13.

35. Jerome, Homilies 42; Prov. 4:8.

36. Jerome, Homilies 48; Ps. 137:8.

37. Jerome, Homilies 59; Ps. 149:3.

38. Eccl. 7:28.

39. Jerome, Letters 107, 13; Eccl. 3:5.

40. Jerome, Letters 123, 13.

41. Prov. 30:15-16.

42. AJ 1, 28.

43. Jerome, Letters 22, 7.

44. Ibid., 48, 20.

45. AJ 1, 28.

46. AJ 1, 30.

47. Jerome, Letters 81, 1.

48. Origen, Commentary on the Song of Songs 1, 4; cf. W. E. Phipps, "The Plight of the Song of Songs," Journal of the American Academy of Religion, Vol. 42 (Mar., 1974), pp. 87-88.

49. Jerome, Letters 22, 25; Song of Songs 4:12.

50. Jerome, Letters 107, 8; Song of Songs 8:10; 5:3.

51. Song of Songs 3:2; 5:6-7.

52. Jerome, Letters 22, 25.

53. Ibid., 22, 26; Song of Songs 5:2; Matt. 25:11-13.

54. Song of Songs 2:1.

55. Jerome, Letters 130, 8.

56. Song of Songs 5:10.

57. AJ 1, 31.

58. Jerome, Letters 22, 41; Song of Songs 2:10.

59. Jerome, Against the Pelagians 3, 13; Song of Songs 4:7.

60. Jerome, Letters 22, 25; Song of Songs 5:4, 8.

61. Jerome, Letters 22, 41; Song of Songs 8:7.

62. AJ 1, 30; Song of Songs 5:1.

63. Jerome, Letters 66, 10; Song of Songs 5:2.

64. Jean Leclecq, The Love of Learning and the Desire for God (New York, 1961), p. 106; cf. John C. Moore, Love in Twelfth-Century France (Philadelphia, 1972), pp. 36-38.

65. Farrar, op. cit., p. 328.

66. Ezek. 24:18.

67. AJ 1, 33.

68. Hosea 13:15.

69. Jerome, Letters 75, 1.

70. Jer. 31:22.

71. AJ 1, 32.

72. Jerome, Letters 22, 19; Dan. 2:45.

73. J. C. Dancy, The Shorter Books of the Apocrypha (Cambridge, 1972), p. 40. Also, in Tobit 6:22 Jerome adds that Tobias is motivated by the duty to procreate rather than by the desire for sex when he does engage in coitus.

74. Ibid., p. 9.

75. Cf. Joseph Kerns, The Theology of Marriage (New York, 1964), pp. 122-123.

76. AJ 1, 25; Luke 1:17.

77. 1 Kings 18:46; 2 Kings 1:8.

78. Jerome, Letters 22, 11.

79. Job 40:16.

80. Jerome, Letters 130, 4.

81. AJ 1, 26.

82. AH 13 and 24.

83. Matt. 1:25.

84. AH 18.

85. AH 6-7; Luke 2:43.

86. AH 8.

87. AH 9; Matt. 13:55-56; Mark 6:3; Luke 2:7.

88. AH 12 and 16; e.g., Gen. 29:15.

89. AH 14 and 17; John 19:25; Mark 15:40.

90. AH 21.

91. Jerome, Letters 48, 21; Song of Songs 4:12; Luke 2:23.

92. Jerome, Against the Pelagians 2, 4; Homilies 87; John 20:19, 26.

93. Jerome, Letters 22, 39; cf. Kelly, op. cit., p. 106.

94. Jerome, Letters 108, 23.

95. Matt. 22:30.

96. AJ 1, 36.

97. Jerome, Letters 108, 23.

98. Matt. 13:8.

99. Jerome, Letters 48, 2; 123, 9.

100. Ibid., 48, 2; 22, 20.

101. AJ 1, 12.

102. Mark 13:17.

103. AJ 1, 12.

104. Jerome, Letters 118, 4.

105. Matt. 19:27.

106. AJ 1, 26.

107. Jerome, Vulgate Bible, Introduction to the Gospel of John.

108. AJ 1, 26.

109. Jerome, Letters 49, 3.

110. Gal. 6:8.

111. AJ 1, 38.

112. Rom. 8:8.

113. AJ 1, 37.

114. Jerome, Letters 130, 2; Rom. 12:1.

115. Gal. 5:22-23.

116. Jerome, Letters 22, 5; 2 Cor. 12:7.

117. E. g., The Letters of Abelard and Heloise, p. 98.

118. Jerome, Against the Pelagians 1, 25; c.f. 1 Cor. 12:34.

119. 1 Cor. 7:5.

120. 1 Thess. 5:17.

121. AJ 1, 7; cf. Jerome, Letters 48, 15.

122. AJ 1, 34.

123. 1 Cor. 7:7.

124. AJ 1, 8.

125. 1 Cor. 7:28.

126. AJ 1, 13.

127. 1 Cor. 7:34.

128. AH 22.

129. AJ 1, 41-49.

130. David S. Wiesen, St. Jerome as a Satirist (New York, 1964), pp. 153-160, 267.

131. Kelly, op. cit., p. 335.

132. E. g., W. E. Phipps, The Sexuality of Jesus (New York, 1973), pp. 53-76.

133. AJ 1, 20.

134. Jerome, Letters 54, 4.

135. AH 22.

136. Geoffrey Chaucer, The Canterbury Tales, 11. 6275-6278.

CHAPTER 3
SEXUAL SHAME IN AUGUSTINE

What in our heritage helps to explain why so many women and men grow up in Christian homes feeling guilty and shameful about having and expressing sexual feelings? Myopic attempts have been made to answer this question by looking backwards only one century to our Victorian ancestors who displayed conflicts even more pronounced. Although clues may be found in the sexually repressive Victorian culture for understanding current phobias, the basic puzzlement remains: how did the Victorians and still earlier generations in Western Christendom come to regard erotic promptings as a sin and a shame? To comprehend the Christian tradition of sexual shame in any adequate way requires that a careful analysis be made of Augustine, the church father who, more than anyone else, molded the prevailing sin-sex syndrome which has affected billions of Christians.

Before going back sixteen centuries to examine Augustine, shame and guilt should be defined and differentiated. Both terms refer to painful feelings resulting from the belief that one has done something wrong, but whereas shame is a reaction of humiliation due to an imagined loss of respect by others, guilt is a self-reproach. David Ausubel offers this clarification: "Shame is a self-deprecatory reaction to the actual or presumed judgment of others....Guilt feelings always involve a special type or moral shame in addition to other negative self-judgments....Thus, the sanctions of guilt are both external and internal in nature."[1] This inquiry will focus more attention on shame, an area much neglected by those analyzing the behavioral pattern of our culture. "Shame is an emotion insufficiently studied," states Erik Erikson, "because in our civilization it is so early and easily absorbed by guilt." That famed psychiatrist describes the emotion of shame in this graphic way: "He who is ashamed would like to force the world not to look at him, not to notice his exposure. He would like to destroy the eyes of the world. Instead he must wish for his own invisibility."[2]

It is not an overstatement to claim that Augustine, who lived most of his life in North Africa during the last years of the ancient Roman empire, has been the most influential Christian leader during the nineteen centuries that separate the biblical era from our contemporary era. That definitive voice of Western Christianity articulated much of the pattern for the Christian conscience that has prevailed for the past millennium and a half. Consequently, a psychosexual examination of Augustine's life can reveal much about the way in which sexuality has been interpreted in the centuries of Roman Catholic and Protestant Christianity that follow. Moreover, since secular culture has also been influenced by religious mores, Augustine's conflicts have been mirrored among many who would not regard themselves as religiously oriented.

Fortunately, there is more information about Augustine's life and times than for any other figure who has lived before the modern era. With him we can get beneath the surface of ancient history and into its inner rhythms. Augustine wrote more than 100 treatises, but it is his Confessions that can afford us the best glimpse into his feelings about sexuality. Recognized as the first introspective autobiography in history, it may provide as much in-depth psychological data as some psychoanalysts can extract from their clients on the couch. Augustine's attitudes toward shame and women will be pieced together by combining insights culled from the Confessions, written in mid-life, with those from a number of his other writings which come mostly from a later period.

Assuming that an adult's sexual outlook is, in considerable part, an outgrowth of values cherished by those who are close to that person in childhood, let us look at Augustine's parents. It is significant that one who lived in a strongly patriarchal culture had little to say about his father, Patricius, but much to say about his mother, Monica. Along with some other Christians and

pagans of her time, she believed that connubial conjunction was
moral only when procreation was desired. However, she could not
persuade her husband to abstain from sexual gratification and so,
in Augustine's words, she "endured the wronging of her bed."[3] The
frigidity of that bed may have stimulated Patricius to find extra-
marital relief. Augustine couples with this infidelity information
another sign of parental incompatibility. Monica avoided facial
disfigurement when Patricius was "violently angry" by always sub-
mitting to him in slavelike obeisance. Lacking a strong affectional
bond with her husband, Monica was especially in need of establishing such with her son.

Augustine first became conscious of his parents' different attitudes toward sex after an episode in a Roman bath. His father proudly
reported to Monica that their boy was displaying signs of sexual matu-
ration. Augustine here accuses his father of "rejoicing in that
tumult of the senses wherein the world forgets Thee its Creator."
This puberty episode caused Monica to tremble with anxiety, for
she interpreted Augustine's fleshly arousal as an outward sign of
evil lust within that might soon lead to fornication.[4] Patricius
may have represented sensuality to Monica inasmuch as she tried to
lure Augustine away from his father: "It was her desire, O my
God, that I should hold you as my father rather than him."[5]

Monica tried, without success, to persuade her son to avoid
sexual involvement. She saw marriage as an interference with her
hopes for his career, but she advised that he should marry young
if his sexual desires "could not be pared away to the quick."[6]
Nevertheless, rebellious Augustine cohabitated with an unnamed
woman for more than a decade and had one son by her.[7] That there
were no more children may have been due to his Manichaean conviction during this period that participation in flesh reproduction
was more evil than engaging in non-procreative sex. The Manichaeans
advocated what has come to be known as the rhythm method of birth
control.[8] Augustine claimed that the relationship with his concubine lacked only the official sanction of marriage,[9] but his now

63

widowed mother regarded the liaison as unconscionable.

When about 30 years old Augustine left Africa for Italy, partly to break away from his domineering mother. "She loved to have me with her," he recalled, "but far more than most mothers." "She followed me to the seacoast and clung to me passionately." Augustine tellingly speaks of the "fleshly affection" (carnale desiderium) that Monica expressed in that frantic farewell.[10] She joined him years later in Milan and persuaded him to cast off his common-law wife in order to become engaged to a girl one-third his age who came from a socially acceptable family.[11] Augustine described that separation in this poignant way: "My heart, to which she clung, was torn and wounded till it bled."[12] However, it does not seem that his emotional attachment resulted in any expression of steadfast concern or support for his dependent wife and young son. He remembered her vow not to remarry but he picked up another concubine to satisfy his "lust" until the girl that Monica selected had reached the marriageable age of twelve.

These autobiographical insights have been rightly interpreted by some scholars as showing narcissism.[13] Psychologist David Bakan gives this somewhat exaggerated appraisal of the evidence: "Augustine was one of the vainest of men because he so sought to concern himself only with himself."[14] Likewise, patrologist Paula Fredriksen observes: "He cannot truly love; his assessment of the nature of sexual love is shaped by his experience of only enjoying a narcissistic gratification from the person loving him."[15]

Monica's fanatical s-mother love was finally victorious, for she lived to see her son take the vow of lifelong celibacy and reject all women except her. After reading a biography of Anthony, a monk who had overcome temptations such as a devilish woman, Augustine prayed, "Give me chastity and self-restraint, but not just yet."[16] This struggle intensified until he had a dramatic peak experience which convinced him to change his lifestyle. Usually the occasion is called Augustine's religious conversion, but it was in large part the settlement of his to-wed-or-not-to-wed dilemma. He expressed the outcome of his experience in this prayer: "You converted me to Thee, so that I sought neither wife nor any ambitions for this world." On learning of this Monica "was filled with triumphant exhilaration."[17] Obviously she was more eager for Augustine to stay single with her than to marry even the upper class bride that she found acceptable. James Dittes has perceptively commented on this: "After years of the most vigorous assertion of his independence, Augustine submitted. He surrendered to his mother, and to her church and to her wishes....He abandoned those things which his father particularly endorsed and represented."[18] Monica could now lavish on her son, without interference from rival women, the intense affection which she withheld from her amorous husband. E. R. Dodds has discussed the Monica-Agustine relationship and discerns that "from this springs his inability to find happiness in the love of women."[19] Shortly before her death she and her son were caught up in a mystical rapture.[20] The "rhythm, flow, and imagery" of that experience strike psychiatrist Charles Kligerman as "passionately orgastic," although he may be overinterpreting the account.[21] Monica's death caused Augustine to feel "torn apart, for it had been one life, made of hers and mine together."[22] Later, as Bishop of Hippo, he asserted that, if it were possible for departed souls to return, she "would not fail to visit me every night, that mother who followed me over land and sea that she might live with me."[23]

Devotion to the Church became a mother-substitute for Augustine. Monica's breast is associated with God's holy temple.[24] In telling about a severe boyhood illness he makes this revealing association: "I begged for baptism...from my mother and from the church, the mother of us all."[25] Peter Brown, in his unsurpassed biography of Augustine, tells how "relentless Monica" functioned like the Church by showing her power to excommunicate her son from her house.[26] As a loyal son of his latter-day mother, Augustine defended the Church from all "heretics" who would violate her. He jealously tried to fend off undesirables from her bosom even as he, as a child, had been "livid with anger while watching another baby at the breast."[27]

Augustine appropriately returned to his mother country and soon became elevated to a secure position in the Church. He lived in monastic seclusion as bishop and followed ecclesiastical etiquette rigorously. F. Van der Meer writes: "No woman might set a foot over the threshold of his house. No woman might speak to him except in the presence of some other person and outside his reception room. He did not even make an exception for his own elder sister."[28]

It appears that Augustine was continent for the remainder of his life, but he was troubled by the awareness that he could not eliminate his sexual urges and the ensuing erections. The good bishop reflects that when he issues a command to his hands or feet, to his eyes or mouth, they instantly obey his will. "To take a still more wonderful case," he muses, "even the liquid contained in the urinary vessels obeys the command to flow."[29] By contrast, the sexual function of the penis is recalcitrant. Augustine exclaims, "Sometimes it refuses to act when the mind wills, while often it acts against its will!"[30] Regarding the former situation he describes further, "Sometimes it abandons the eager lover and desire cools off in the body while it is at boiling heat in the mind."[31]

Women were, for Augustine, the incarnation of seductiveness, and a holy man should avoid them as he avoids the devil. He was convinced that "nothing so casts down the manly mind from its heights as the fondling of women and those bodily contacts which belong to the married state."[32] Yet he admits that he, in his unmarried state, was little better off. He evaluates as "vile, detestable, shameful, and dreadful" the sexual fantasies in which he indulged.[33] After many years of celibate life he prayed: "More and more, Lord, increase your gifts in me, so that my soul may be freed from the bird-lime of lust. May it rebel no more by the sensual images of dreams which cause debasing acts of turpitude that result in the pollution of the flesh."[34]

The sexual fears of both Monica and Augustine were, of course, much influenced by the mores of their era. Augustine grew to manhood during a time when monasticism was developing and when interest in renouncing wine, women, and meat was pronounced. Those ascetic practices were the outcome of a moral dualism principle that was commonplace among Greco-Roman cults. On the assumption that the physical was bad, Platonic, Manichaean, and Christian leaders advised people to liberate their spirits by reducing material consumption to a mere survival level. The ideal lifestyle was that of the Stoic sage who aimed at eliminating his passions in order to become totally rational.[35]

The sexual pattern of Augustine's private life and social era heavily tinted his interpretations of Scripture. He projected his frustrations over penis control by attempting to denigrate women far more than the Hebrews had done. The Creator made women's minds inferior to men's, he believed.[36] Looking at Genesis 1 through the distorting lens of Paul, Augustine declared: "Woman is not the image of God, for man alone is that image."[37] Even in the perfect Eden state of humankind "it cannot be doubted that it is more consonant with the order of nature that men should bear rule over women, than women over men."[38] Lacking authority, women cannot govern, teach, or witness in court.[39] Both the "Fall of man" and the subsequent catastrophic flood were occasioned by unruly women. Even though the Genesis flood story does not single out women for blame, Augustine alleged that it was their "depraved morals" and "physical beauty" that precipitated that second calamity.[40] Monica was faithful to Augustine's Bible in telling other women that they should not "rise up against their lord and master."[41]

Since sexual desire was for Augustine the principal springboard for plunging into sin, he postulates that it could not have been a part of God's perfect creation. Why then was there in Eden sexual differentiation at all? Woman was created exclusively to enable man to fulfill God's command to populate the earth,

Augustine reflects:

> If it is asked why this helper was created, it is probable that
> there is no other reason than for the generation of children,
> just as the earth is a help for the seed....For if woman were
> not created...to produce children, for what other help would
> she be made? If also to till the earth, it must be answered
> that there was no laborious task for which man needed her
> help, and if there were, a man would be a better helper. The
> same can be said of companionship if the man perhaps were
> bored with his solitude. For how much more fitting for com-
> mon life and conversation would it be if two male friends
> rather than a man and woman lived together?...Therefore, I
> cannot see how woman should be made a help to man except by
> childbearing.[42]

If Adam had not sinned, he would have fertilized Eve while
relaxing on her bosom without the goading of passion. His mind
would coolly have summoned his semen forth and, without hymenal
impairment, it would have dripped down into her vagina.[43] "Away
with the thought that there should have been...any unregulated
excitement," Augustine insists.[44] To show that it is plausible to
think that man could have had complete bodily control in his un-
corrupted condition, Augustine tells of the remarkable control
that some individuals have over bodily parts other than the penis:

> There are persons who can move their ears, either one at a
> time, or both together....Some have such command of their
> bowels that they can fart whenever they please so as to
> produce a musical effect. I myself have known a man who was
> accustomed to sweat whenever he wished....Seeing, then, that
> even in this mortal and miserable life the body serves some
> men by many remarkable movements and moods beyond the ordinary
> course of nature, what reason is there for doubting that,
> before man was involved by his sin in this weak and corruptible
> condition, his members might have served his will for the prop-
> agation of offspring without lust?...At that time those
> private parts were not moved by the turbulence of lust.[45]

Only after indulging in sin was Adam unable to keep his penis
from acting up. It became like a domestic animal that had rebelled
against obedience training and would not respond to its owner's
commands.[46] Augustine thought that Adam received a fitting
penalty for willful disobedience to the fruit tree prohibition in
having his penis become likewise disobedient to his will. Adam,

who had previously been naked and unashamed, now is highly embarrassed at the "bestial motion" of his penis.[47] Indeed, blushing,
a physiological expression of shame, originated in mankind from
Adam's chagrin over penile perversity.[48] He quickly covers his
loins in order to conceal from others that he no longer has total
self-mastery.[49] Power over the penis is lost forever to Adam's
offspring and henceforth its arousal and its orgasm will often be
triggered by someone else. Eve as well as Adam was conscience-
stricken by her involuntary sexual impulses. "The motion of their
bodily members," Augustine writes, "released the shocking news of
their indecent nakedness, made them notice it, and gave them
shame."[50]

Augustine maintains that all humans who have been conceived
by sexual intercourse inherit from Adam unruly genitals. He tells
men in his congregation that each can witness the effect of the
Fall in his penis' disobedience to authoritative command and can
realize that the corrupted semen ejaculated from the faulty member
will contaminate the next generation. "Behold the place!" he
exclaims; "That's the place from which the first sin is passed
on."[51] Augustine regards the term pudenda (from Latin, meaning
"something to be ashamed of") to be an apt one for the genitals
"because they excite themselves, just as they like, in opposition
to the mind which should be their master."[52] He finds further
evidence of the perpetual shameful consequence of Adam's sin in
the fact that couples, even when bound in legal wedlock, dread
engaging in intercourse except in a dark place. "Even shameless
men call this shameful," Augustine claims; "and though they love
the pleasure, dare not display it."[53] Consequently, married partners

> seek out secret retreats for cohabitation, and dare not have
> even the children whom they have themselves begotten to be
> witnesses of what they do. It was against this modesty of
> natural shame that the Cynic philosophers, in the error of
> their astonishing shamelessness, struggled so hard; they
> thought that the intercourse indeed of husband and wife, since
> it was lawful and honorable, should therefore be done in

public. Such brazen obscenity deserved to receive the name of dogs; and so they went by the title of "Cynics."[54]

International bathing practices are cited by Augustine as another proof of the universal sexual shame that has resulted from the sin of Adam and Eve. In his major treatise, City of God, he writes, "Shame modestly covered that which lust disobediently moved in opposition to the will, which was thus punished for its own disobedience. Consequently all nations, being propagated from that one stock, have so strong an instinct to cover the shameful parts that some foreigners do not uncover them even in the bath, but wash with their drawers on."[55]

While admitting that sexual consummation produces "the greatest of all bodily pleasures,"[56] Augustine believed it was dishonorable for Christians to seek sexual pleasure even within marriage. Marital coitus can be engaged in without commiting "venial" sin only if spouses are exclusively motivated by a grim determination to propagate.[57] "Since you cannot reproduce in any other way," he laments, "you must descend against your will to this punishment of Adam."[58] The bishop advises a man to love his wife as he loves his enemy--he should accept both as creatures of God but hate what makes them corrupt. With respect to the latter, a husband should hate his spouse's desire for sexual pleasure.[59] In his several treatises on marriage the sexual act as a symbolic expression of devoted love is nowhere regarded as even a secondary purpose of marriage. Augustine argues that it is wrong for married couples who do not hope for conception to have sexual union even as it is wrong for a person to consume food in excess of what is necessary for survival.[60]

To renounce sexual intercourse entirely was to hasten the coming of the perfected City of God.[61] Consequently Augustine praises those already bound in matrimony who have vowed "to observe a perpetual abstinence from the use of carnal concupiscence."[62] He pictured the ideal wedded life as one undisturbed by sexual passion, probably due to his mother's influence. Likewise he commended the supererogation of virginal men and women who imposed upon themselves the command, "Thou shalt not wed."[63]

One of Augustine's favorite biblical passages, which he quotes
hundreds of times, is a confession of the apostle Paul. In treating the turmoil of his divided self, Paul admits: "Sin dwells in
my members."[64] By "members" Paul had reference to his entire
alienated self, but Augustine presumed to find here a specific
reference to the male member and thought that the apostle was discussing the impotence of the will to keep the penis docile.

Augustine regarded Jesus as the "last Adam" to whom Paul
referred[65] who, like the first Adam before his Fall, had no sexual
drive. The bishop believed that God effected this unique exception
to the rest of humanity by miraculously enabling a woman to become
fertilized without the contaminated semen of Adam's descendants.[66]
Whereas the first Adam was "able not to sin," Jesus, because of his
virginal conception, was "not able to sin."[67]

In his scheme of sin and salvation, Augustine regarded man's
rambunctious private parts as proof of his being conceived in
iniquity and of his being normally destined for the torment of
hell. Jesus, the lustless Savior, rescues some who would other-
wise receive their just damnation. Those few whom God elects
should show their appreciation by attempting to imitate the lifestyle which Jesus allegedly had. Augustine's doctrine did much to
attract guilt-stricken people to the medieval monasteries where
sexual discipline was prominently featured.

Thomas Aquinas, the most famous medieval follower of Augustine, accepted virtually all of his mentor's attitudes toward
sexuality. Presupposing that Augustine's description of women was
true, Aquinas protected his virtue by staying clear of them.
Regarding the genitals, he writes: "It is in punishment of sin
that the movement of these members does not obey reason. That is
to say, the soul is punished for its rebellion against God by
the insubmission of that member whereby original sin is transmitted
to posterity."[68] Like Augustine, that "Angelic Doctor" of Roman
Catholicism believed that woman was created only to help him

reproduce.[69] Since procreation was for him the sina qua non of
sexual expression, Aquinas judged autoerotic or homosexual acts to
be graver sins than rape or incest. The former were classified as
unnatural sins because procreation is impossible, whereas rape and
incest are natural sins because conception may result.[70]

The impact of Augustine and Aquinas on shame reactions toward
autoerotic practice has been enormous. The very word "masturbatio,"
the traditional and still commonplace term to describe this activity,
expresses the negative moral judgment given in Latin Christianity.
"Masturbation" is a compound word which probably comes from the
Latin terms for "hand" (manus) and "defilement" (stuprum). Orgasms
produced either by manual stimulation or involuntarily, by what
churchmen have called "nocturnal pollutions," have both been regarded as shameful. As a result of medieval Christianity it has
been widely believed for many centuries that this so-called "self-
abuse" causes such dreaded effects as acne, feeblemindedness, and
infertility.[71] The assumption here is that sexual expression is
perverted and punished by God if it is not used in a way to make
reproduction possible. Since masturbation is the first genital
sexual expression for most children, parental proscription of the
practice effectively transmits from generation to generation the
Augustinian linkage between sin and sexual pleasure.

Martin Luther, although he left his Augustinian monastic order, retained much of Augustine's outlook on sexual shame. In his
commentary on Genesis, Luther wrote that due to the Fall "the
glory of the genitals was turned into the utmost disgrace, so that
man was compelled to cover them with a girdle."[72] Soren Kierkegaard,
a follower of Luther three centuries after the Protestant Reformation, accepted the Augustinian view of sexuality. That gloomy
Danish philosopher thought of the human physical urges as Pandora's
box, filled with the basic ills of human existence, and he spent
his life trying to fasten shut the lid of his id. Kierkegaard's
sexual revulsion resulted from some personal experiences as well
as from the Augustinian tradition. As he grew up he discovered

that he had been conceived in adultery by a family servant shortly before his father's first wife died. His dread of sex was increased by fornicating at a brothel when intoxicated. Consequently he broke with his fiance Regina and became a celibate, believing that total dedication to God demanded abstaining from the satisfaction of sexual desires.[73] After having rather unusual personal sexual encounters, both Augustine and Kierkegaard presumed that their shame reaction was due to physical inheritance from Adam. They blamed universal human nature rather than particular family nurture for their neuroses.

The dark shadow of the towering Augustine is still upon us in modern times. Anglican scholar Sherwin Bailey rightly charges: "Augustine must bear no small measure of responsibility for the insinuation into our culture of the idea, still widely current, that Christianity regards sexuality as something peculiarly tainted with evil."[74] Again, Greek Orthodox theologian Demosthenes Savramis observes:

> Augustine's inability to manage his own sexual problems provided the basis of a theology that decisevely influence the so-called Christian West. His theology of sexuality, which I am inclined to call genitocentric, views the phallus as independent from man's total personality, even as his enemy....He could hardly imagine that religion and sexuality might coexist.[75]

One of the many examples of Augustinianism in the twentieth century is found in the writings of the eminent Swiss theologian Emil Brunner. He writes:

> Man is not merely ashamed of the sexuality which is forbidden to him morally, but shame accompanies him even into the completely personal sex-relation in marriage, and indeed the more he determines himself as person, the more spiritual his existence, the more is he aware of this. We cannot think of our Lord as married, although we are not in the least jarred by the fact that he ate and drank like the rest of mankind.[76]

Popular treatments of the history of Western sexuality often use the label "Puritan" to refer to a repressive sexual morality, when "Augustinian" would be the more accurate term. Puritan leaders, such as John Calvin and John Milton, were much more accepting of the goodness of sexuality than most of the Christians who have lived in the centuries preceding or following them.[77]

In contrast to the Augustinian view of shame, the dominant biblical view on the intrinsic shamelessness of sexuality will be sketched. The Eve and Adam story introduces well that viewpoint: there sexual partnership is viewed as a divinely ordained relief from the less-than-satisfactory solitary state. Seeing the woman evokes this passionate response from the man: "At last, here is one of my own kind." Prior to the entrance of the serpent, the nude couple engage in a "one flesh" marital union and it is stated that they had no feeling of shame towards one another. Thus the shame that follows stealing fruit is due not to sexual passion and its expression but to an awareness of having broken faith with the Creator.[78] This embarrassment causes the couple to engage in frantic but futile attempts to lessen their vulnerability to the Lord from whom they are alienated. Calvin captures the naiveté of the story with this comment: "They sew together for themselves girdles of leaves. For what end? That they may keep God at a dis-tance, as by an invincible barrier!"[79] They not only covered themselves but they also hide behind the trees in Eden. Moreover, when questioned by God, Adam tried to hide behind Eve, and Eve behind the serpent.

Elsewhere in Genesis the male sexual organs are afforded high honor. Abraham has his servant make a vow by placing his hand on his master's genitals in much the same way as the Bible has been used for oath-taking in courtrooms.[80] Thus there is biblical justification for deriving both the terms testicle and testimony from the same Latin root testis. Also, the penis is selected as the part of the body on which to place the seal of the sacred covenant with Abraham. Cutting around its glans was like uncorking the bottle of god-given virility and permitting its flow to provide for the continued existence of the "chosen people." Thus the penis symbolized new life and the patriarchs thought of themselves as co-workers with the Creator when they used it. Although it could be misused for sordid purposes, it was principally thought

74

of as an instrument for accomplishing a sacred purpose.

Again, joy is a more appropriate term than shame to describe the mood of Isaac when he fondled his lovely wife. There is a punny remark in a sermon by a seventeenth century Puritan about this uxorious play" "Marriage doth signifie merry-age, because a play-fellow is come to make our age merry, as Isaak and Rebecca sported together."[81]

The biblical view of the innocence of marital sexuality is most beautifully expressed in the Song of Songs. It continues the Eden ode to marital sexuality and shows that an alleged "Fall" has not corrupted human love. The bride and groom have no feeling of shame as they adore and explore one another's naked bodies. They blend together all the senses in order to heighten their exhilaration--fragrant spices, endearing words, anatomical viewing, graceful dancing, bird-song listening, and tender kisses. Here is a sampling of the way sexual desire ("lust") is expressed by a bridegroom, and the way his partner responds:

>"You are stately as a palm-tree,
>and your breasts are the clusters of dates...."
>"I am my beloved's, his longing is all for me.
>Come, my beloved, let us go out into the fields
>to lie among the henna-bushes."[82]

Augustine and many other churchmen have falsified the original meaning of the Song by claiming that it has nothing to do with erotic love.[83] However, that most passionate of all ancient songs should be read as a testimony to the goodness of natural desires.

The New Testament continues the viewpoint of Jewish Scriptures on the shamelessness of marital intercourse. When Jesus was asked for his opinion on what the marriage bond should be, he referred back to the Genesis story which tells of the unashamedly naked first couple who linked together their loins.[84] The main shame of which the New Testament speaks pertains to the crucifixion of an innocent man, not the embarrassment over the loss of orgastic control. However, it does not consider shame as an inappropriate response to illicit sexual activity. Thus Paul judges prostitution, along with to be shameful.[85]

Augustine might well have inculcated the outlook of his older contemporary, Gregory Nazianzen, whom he highly respected. That Archbishop of Constantinople was disturbed that "most men have a tendency that is most unreasonable,...unfair, and inconsistent" in dealing with sexual matters. They are, he points out, severe in judging the opposite sex and lenient in dealing with themselves. Thus they heap upon women guilt that is unjust. Gregory then reminds his congregation that "the woman sinned, and so did Adam. The serpent deceived them both; one was not found to be the stronger and the other the weaker....The two, Christ says, shall be one flesh; so let the one flesh have equal honor....Let the wife, Paul says, see that she reverence her husband, for so she does Christ; but also he bids the husband cherish his wife, for so Christ does the church."[86] Sexual shame, which has been heavy on men but even more oppressive on women, is in part due to failure to give "equal honor" to the sexes. When woman is regarded by Augustine and others as inferior then intimate relations with her involves a shameful loss of dignity.

There are a number of commendable theological and philosophical positions in Augustine's thought, but in the area of sexuality he did a great disservice to the religion of the Bible that he professed to admire. There are encouraging signs that many religious people are now extricating themselves from Augustinian sexual shame and are recovering a more healthy outlook toward their bodies. Evidence of this is seen in the responses to a sex questionnaire circulated widely among American women. According to the recently published report on the questionnaire results, "the more religious a woman described herself as being, the happier she said she was with her sex life and her marriage."[87] This suggests that the Augustinian emphasis on sexual shame is at last being replaced by a viewpoint that is more in line with the original biblical viewpoint on sexual pleasure.

NOTES

1. David Ausubel, "Relationships Between Shame and Guilt in the Socializing Process," Psychological Review 62 (1955), p. 389.

2. Erik Erikson, Childhood and Society (New York, 1963), pp. 252-253.

3. Augustine, Confessions 9, 19.

4. Ibid., 2, 6.

5. Ibid., 1, 17.

6. Ibid., 2, 7-8.

7. Ibid., 4, 2.

8. Augustine, On the Morals of the Manichaeans 65.

9. Augustine, Confessions, 6, 22.

10. Ibid., 5, 15.

11. Ibid., 6, 23.

12. Ibid., 6, 25.

13. James Dittes, "Continuities Between the Life and Thought of Augustine," Journal for the Scientific Study of Religion 5 (1965), p. 135; Paul Pruyser, "Psychological Examination: Augustine," Journal for the Scientific Study of Religion 5 (1966), p. 288.

14. David Bakan, "Some Thoughts on Reading Augustine's Confessions," Journal for the Scientific Study of Religion 5 (1965), p. 150.

15. Paula Fredriksen, "Augustine and his Analysts," Soundings 61 (1978), p. 222.

16. Augustine, Confessions 8, 17.

17. Ibid., 8, 30.

18. James Dittes, op. cit., p. 137.

19. E. R. Dodds, "Augustine's Confessions: A Study of Spiritual Maladjustment," Hibbert Journal 26 (1928), p. 466.

20. Augustine, Confessions 9, 10.

21. Charles Kligerman, "A Psychoanalytic Study of the Confessions of St. Augustine," Journal of the American Psychoanalytic Association 5 (1957), p. 483; cp. Fredriksen, op. cit., p. 211.

22. Augustine, Confessions 9, 30.

23. Augustine, The Care to Be Taken for the Dead 13, 16.

24. Augustine, Confessions 2, 6.
25. Ibid., 1, 17.
26. Peter Brown, Augustine of Hippo (Berkeley, 1969), p. 406; cf. Confessions 3, 19.
27. Ibid., 1, 11.
28. F. Van der Meer, Augustine the Bishop (London, 1961), p. 215.
29. Augustine, On Marriage and Concupiscence 2, 53.
30. Ibid., 1, 7.
31. Augustine, City of God 14, 16.
32. Augustine, Soliloquies 1, 17.
33. Ibid., 1, 25.
34. Augustine, Confessions 10, 42.
35. Cf. William E. Phipps, Was Jesus Married? (New York, 1970), pp. 120-163.
36. Augustine, Commentary on Genesis 3, 22, 34; 9, 2, 4.
37. Augustine, On the Trinity, 12, 7, 10.
38. Augustine, On Marriage and Concupiscence 1, 10.
39. Augustine, Questions on the Old Testament, 21.
40. Augustine, City of God 15, 22; cp. Gen. 6:1-4.
41. Augustine, Confessions 9, 19.
42. Augustine, Commentary on Genesis 9, 5, 9.
43. Augustine, City of God 14, 26.
44. Augustine, Against Two Letters of the Pelagians 1, 34.
45. Augustine, City of God 14, 24. Surely this must rank as one of the most bizarre extrapolations in the history of theology!
46. Ibid., 14, 19.
47. Augustine, On Original Sin 39-43.
48. Augustine, Against Two Letters of the Pelagians 1, 33.
49. Augustine, On Marriage and Concupiscence 1, 7.
50. Augustine, City of God 14, 17.
51. Augustine, Sermons 151, 5; cf. Brown, op. cit., p. 388.
52. Augustine, On Forgiveness of Sins 2, 36.
53. Augustine, City of God 14, 18.
54. Augustine, On Marriage and Concupiscence 1, 24.

55. Augustine, City of God 14, 17.

56. Ibid., 14, 16.

57. Augustine, On the Good of Marriage 11.

58. Augustine, Sermons 51, 15.

59. Augustine, The Sermon on the Mount 1, 15, 41.

60. Augustine, On the Good of Marriage 18.

61. Ibid., 10.

62. Augustine, On Marriage and Concupiscence 12; On Original Sin 41.

63. Augustine, On the Good of Marriage 30.

64. Rom. 7:23; Henri Marrou, St. Augustine (New York, 1958), p. 84, states that Paul quotes Rom. 7:22-25 at least 225 times.

65. 1 Cor. 15:45.

66. Augustine, On Marriage and Concupiscence 2, 14.

67. Augustine, Unfinished Work Against Julian 6, 22.

68. Aquinas, Summa Theologica 1-2, q. 17, 9.

69. Ibid., 1, q. 154, 12.

70. Aquinas, op. cit., 2-2, q. 154, 12.

71. Cf. William E. Phipps, "Masturbation: Vice or Virtue?," Journal of Religion and Health, July, 1977, pp. 183-193.

72. Jaroslav Pelikan, ed. Luther's Works (St. Louis, 1958) 1, p. 168.

73. Cf. William E. Phipps, The Sexuality of Jesus (New York, 1973), pp. 89-91.

74. D. Sherwin Bailey, Sexual Relation in Christian Thought (New York, 1959), p. 59.

75. Demosthenes Savramis, The Satanizing of Woman (New York, 1974), p. 50.

76. Emil Brunner, Man in Revolt (Philadelphia, 1947), p. 348.

77. Cf. Phipps, The Sexuality of Jesus, pp. 99-103.

78. Cf. John Skinner, A Critical and Exegetical Commentary on Genesis (New York, 1917), p. 76.

79. John Calvin, Commentaries (Grand Rapids, 1948) 1, p. 159.

80. Gen. 17:10-14; 24:1-4.

81. Henry Smith, The Sermons of Master Henry Smith (London, 1628), p. 12; Gen. 26:8.

82. Song of Songs 6:7, 10-11. (New English Bible)
83. Cf. William E. Phipps, Recovering Biblical Sensuousness (Philadelphia, 1975), pp. 44-66.
84. Mark 10:7-8; Gen. 2:24-25.
85. Eph. 5:3-12.
86. Gregory Nazianzen, Orations 37, 6-7.
87. Carol Tavris and Susan Sadd, The Redbook Report on Female Sexuality (New York, 1977), p. 98.

It is becoming apparent that valuable insights into the
Christian tradition can be found by examining the outlook on
women held by pivotal churchmen. Consideration will now be given
to John Knox who is venerated by members of the Reformed churches
in Britain and in America as their earliest and most influential
English-speaking leader. Episodes pertaining to women in the life
of that sixteenth century figure will be described in chronological
sequence and then general comments will be made on their significance.

Little is known about Knox's youth other than that he came
from a humble background to study for the priesthood at St. Andrews,
the ecclesiastical capital of Scotland.[1] Although he left the
"puddle of papistry"[2] at the beginning of the fourth decade of his
life, he remained a bachelor for another decade.

The first information on record of Knox's involvement with
women comes from the several years that he was a parish minister
in the English town of Berwick on the Scottish border. There he
encountered Elizabeth Bowes, the neurotic wife of a well-to-do
country gentleman and the mother of fifteen children. Having found
that Catholicism gave her no peace of mind, she searched, with
little success, for assurance of salvation in the Reformed faith.
Knox frequently reassured her that she need not have such a
troubled conscience. Once, for example, when she accused herself
of having committed the sin of Sodom, he pointed out that not
"every ardent and burning lust" deserves that label. Again,
Mrs. Bowes informed her confessor that she had doubts about the
biblical story of creation. Knox responded that the pain which
women have in childbirth verifies what is recorded in Genesis.[3]

Knox was charmed by having this woman with social standing
seek his advice. His remarks to Mrs. Bowes, which have been
preserved in 29 letters, display that their relationship was
closer than what would be normal in pastoral counselling. Once he

wrote: "Call to mind what I did standing at the cupboard at
Alnwick. In very deed I thought that no creature had been tempted
as I was."[4] He came to realize that the extended sessions they
were having together were causing criticism. So he confessed that
he was sad "that such as most gladly would remain together for
mutual comfort cannot be allowed so to do." He continued: "Since
the first day that it pleased the providence of God to bring you
and me in familiarity I have always delighted in your company and,
when labor would permit, you know I have not spared hours to talk
and commune with you."[5] Knox learned that he needed to restrain
his written communication as well: "The slander and fear of men
has impeded me to exercise my pen so oft as I would," he wrote;
"yes very shame has held me from your company."[6]

Mrs. Bowes was resourceful in scheming a way for this companionship to continue with propriety. She advised Knox to marry her
fifteen year daughter, Marjorie; then, as mother-in-law, it would
be altogether proper for her to visit where Knox resided. He
attempted to carry out this plan but found Mr. Bowes not at all
willing to give his daughter to an aging, defrocked priest of low
birth. Knox wrote Mrs. Bowes that he would persevere with the
negotiation: "It becomes me now to jeopard my life for the comfort
and deliverance of my own flesh."[7]

Meanwhile Knox accepted a parish in London and became a royal
chaplain to Edward VI. There he became friendly with several women
and closely attached to Anne Locke, the wife of a prominent
Protestant merchant with whom he was living.[8] She was a learned
woman who shared more of Knox's social concerns than Mrs. Bowes
was able to do.

After the untimely death of Edward, Knox was afraid to remain
in England. Mary Tudor, the Catholic successor to the throne, had
instigated Protestant persecutions. At that time Mrs. Bowes wrote
Knox urging that her marital scheme be pursued further, so he
tried again to secure Mr. Bowes' acquiescence in his daughter's
marriage to a poor preacher. The father's resistance to this

match--and perhaps Marjorie's as well--was as firm as several years earlier. Although Knox left England without a bride, he soon returned and eloped to Geneva with both Marjorie and her mother.[9] Judging from the fact that Mr. Bowes did not mention either his wife or Marjorie in his will,[10] it can be concluded that he never approved of their attachment to Knox. Mrs. Bowes not only deserted her husband but also left behind several young unmarried daughters. In a perceptive essay on Knox's private life, Robert Louis Stevenson comments:

> It is easy enought to understand the anger of Bowes against this interloper, who had come into a quiet family, married the daughter in spite of the father's opposition, alienated the wife from the husband and the husband's religion, supported her in a long course of resistance and rebellion, and, after years of intimacy, already too close and tender for any jealous spirit to behold without resentment, carried her away with him at last into a foreign land.[11]

Little is known about Knox's relationship with Marjorie. Only one letter addressed to her has been preserved and even that letter is largely devoted to her mother's troubles. Knox rarely mentioned his wife in his many long letters to Mrs. Bowes, so it can be assumed that Marjorie counted for little to either of them. She gave birth to two sons while living in Geneva and died at the age of 25 in Edinburgh. Mrs. Bowes continued to live with her son-in-law after Marjorie's death, and this questionable relationship renewed gossip about incestuous conduct. Both Knox and his critics were concerned about the biblical prohibition which states: "If a man takes both a wife and her mother, it is wickedness; both he and they shall be burnt."[12] Consequently, the last tract that Knox published before his death contained a claim that his relationship with his mother-in-law had been a spiritual, not a fleshly one.[13]

Not long after Mrs. Bowes and her daughter came to live in Geneva, Knox wrote Mrs. Locke that he yearned for her. "If I should express the thirst and languor which I have had for your presence," he disclosed, "I should appear to pass measure."[14]

Moved by that passionate appeal, she left her husband to live in
Knox's household. While in Geneva Mrs. Locke wrote to Knox, who
was away in France, to chide him for his negligence in correspondence.
He responded: "My remembrance of you is not so dead, but I trust
it shall be fresh enough, albeit it be renewed by no outward token
for one year. Of nature, I am churlish:...yet one thing I ashame
not to affirm that familiarity once thoroughly contracted was never
yet broken on my default."[15] Patrick Collinson, who has made an
extensive study of Anne Locke's life, has concluded that "no one
was ever closer" to Knox than she was.[16] In his 13 extant letters
to her there is hardly any mention of her husband. However,
Mr. Locke was faithful to his wife and when he died his entire
estate was bequeathed to her.[17]

Knox seems to have approved of the separation of wives from
husbands only if he was the beneficiary. While Mrs. Locke and
Mrs. Bowes were both living with him, he wrote to Mrs. McGill, a
Scottish friend, who was having marital difficulties with her
husband. Knox told her that even though her "enemy" spouse has
"coldness which justly may be called infidelity," she should remain
with him. In that letter Knox also remarked that "the prophets of
God are oft impeded to pray for such as carnally they love."[18]
In another letter Knox described a "wicked and rebellious woman"
who was guilty of "unlawful departing from her husband" and of
withdrawing from her home country.[19]

While Knox was surrounded in his Geneva household by devoted
women--Mrs. Locke, Mrs. Bowes, and Marjorie--he thought through
his position on the status of women. In sixteenth century England
there had been considerable reexamination of traditional views on
woman's place. Cornelius Agrippa, for example, in a treatise
published in London in 1542 defended women as being in every
respect equal, or superior, to men. "In ruling of realms and
building of cities women excel," he wrote.[20] James Phillips, after
citing a number of English books published during this period with
a similar outlook, concludes: "For the most part, the Renaissance

Englishman was fulsome in his praise and defense of the opposite sex."[21]

The critics of traditional female stereotypes provoked a heated controversy in the decade before Knox wrote his tract on women. Edward Gosynill's Schole House of Women became popular even though it surely must rank as one of the vilest misogynistic writings ever published. In it gynecocratic advocates are denounced by showing that selected passages of the Bible and the church fathers prove that women are inferior.[22] Since Knox was soon to treat Eve, Jezebel, and some other biblical women in a similarly contemptuous manner, it may be that he had read Gosynill's propaganda.

The issue of the rule of women was not a theoretical one for Knox. He was irked that his work in England had been halted by the reign of Mary Tudor. Then, in his home country, Mary of Guise (or, of Lorraine) was the regent for her daughter, Mary Stewart (or Stuart). In addition, there was another woman in France, Catherine de Medici, who was soon to become regent. Knox's contempt for these women was compounded by the fact that they were Catholics and that there was selective persecution of Protestants in each of the three countries.

Years of consideration were given by Knox to the question of women rulers before he articulated his own position. He took advantage of the opportunity afforded him in Switzerland by consulting with the two best minds in the Reformed church, John Calvin and Henry Bullinger. To each he raised the question of "whether a female can preside over, and rule a kingdom by divine right." Calvin told Knox in 1554 that although gynecocracy was contrary to the normal course of nature, "the grace of God sometimes displays itself in an extraordinary way, since, as a reproach to the sloth of men, he raises up women, endowed not after the nature of men, but with a certain heroic spirit, as is seen in the illustrious example of Deborah."[23] Calvin, who endorsed resistance to rulers only when led by a constituted assembly,[24] went on to assert that political rebellion is not the right of a private-citizen.

Evidently not satisfied with his mentor's position on this matter, Knox raised the same issue in a letter to Bullinger. That Zurich reformer replied that the Bible ordains that women not rule. However, if a woman by state law does rule, godly people should not rebel, for "the Lord will in his own time destroy unjust government."[25]

The only leader whom we know to have agreed with Knox was Christopher Goodman, his closest male friend. Once Goodman was referred to by Knox as one "whose presence I more thirst than she that is my own flesh."[26] These men were co-pastors of the church for English exiles in Geneva and each published at Geneva in 1558 tracts on the rule of women. Goodman wrote: "God...at the beginning appointed the woman to be in subjection to her husband, as said the Apostle who will not permit so much to the woman as to speak in the assembly of men, much less to be ruler of a realm or nation."[27] His logic, which Knox also endorsed, was that it is absurd to give the office of highest responsibility in the state to a woman when she is not considered competent to perform the lesser offices of judge, teacher, and the like.

Knox, perhaps realizing that his radical position would have to be well argued to be persuasive, put much scholarly labor into his work entitled The First Blast of the Trumpet Against the Monstrous Regiment of Women. It compares favorably with the scholasticism of Thomas Aquinas in orderliness of argument. He drew on the writings of some church fathers that he encountered when studying for the priesthood, and on his biblical studies after becoming a Reformed clergyman.

In the preface of the tract Knox states that the encouragement to rebel is being written primarily for the common people and not for the nobility. Then, after giving his subtitle, "The First Blast to Awake Women Degenerate," he presents the thesis he plans to defend. In the main body of his tract he quotes and paraphrases extensively from philosophical and religious literature. With regard to the latter he proceeds chronologically from the Old Testament, to the New Testament, and then to the Latin and Greek fathers of the church. In the last part of the tract Knox responds to anticipated objections. He rejects the argument which Calvin and Aquinas[28] advanced, that giving temporal authority to women was sanctioned by God because of the precedent of Deborah's rule in Bible times. Knox contends that Israel was in a state of apostasy when she was a judge, so her tribal leadership has no bearing on proper civil government.

Excerpts from the First Blast, that display the sequence of Knox's argument, follow:

[Preface:] Of necessity it is that this monstriferous empire of women (which among all enormities that this day do abound upon the face of the whole earth, is most detestable and damnable) be openly revealed and plainly declared to the world, to the end that some may repent and be saved....To such as think that it will be long before such doctrine come to the ears of the chief offenders, I answer that...we are debters to more than to princes, to wit, to the multitude of our brethren....

[Thesis:] To promote a woman to bear rule, superiority, dominion, or empire, above any realm, nation, or city, is repugnant to nature, contumely to God, a thing most contrarious to his revealed will and approved ordinance; and finally, it is the subversion of good order, of all equity and justice....

Nature...paints women...to be weak, frail, impatient, feeble, and foolish; and experience has declared them to be inconstant, variable, cruel, and lacking the spirit of counsel and government....

Aristotle...plainly affirms that wherever women bear dominion the people will be disordered, living and abounding in all intemperance, given to pride, excess, and vanity; and finally, they will come to confusion and ruin....

Woman in her greatest perfection knew that man was lord above her; and therefore she never pretended any kind of superiority above him, no more than do the angels above God.... But after her fall and rebellion committed against God, there was put upon her a new necessity, and she was made subject to man by the irrevocable sentence of God, pronounced in these words:..."Your will shall be subject to your husband, and he shall bear dominion over you." As if God should say, "Forasmuch as you have abused your former condition, and because your free will has brought yourself

87

and mankind into the bondage of Satan, I therefore will bring
you in bondage to man. For where before your obedience
should have been voluntary, now it shall be by constraint and
by necessity; and that because you have deceived your man,
you shall therefore be no longer ruler over your own appetites,
over your own will or desires. For in you there is neither
reason nor discretion which is able to moderate your affections,
and therefore they shall be subject to the desire of your man.
He shall be lord and governor, not only over your body, but
even over your appetites and will." This sentence, I say,
did God pronounce against Eve and her daughters, as the rest
of the Scriptures does witness....So that woman by the law of
God, and by the interpretation of the Holy Ghost, is utterly
forbidden to occupy the place of God in the offices...which he
has assigned to man, whom he has appointed and ordained his
lieutenant on earth, excluding from that honor and dignity
all women, as this short argument shall declare.

The Apostle took power from all women to speak in the
assembly; therefore, he permitted no woman to rule above man....
For he that takes from woman the least part of authority,
dominion, or rule, will not permit unto her that which is
greatest....

[Tertullian held that for women] it is no more possible
that she being set aloft in authority above man shall resist
the motions of pride, than it is able for the weak reed, or
for the turning weathercock, not to bow or turn at the vehemency
of the inconstant wind. And therefore the same writer
expressly forbade all women to meddle with the office of man....

[Augustine asked:] "How can woman be the image of God,
seeing she is subject to man, and has no authority to teach,
or to be witness, or to judge, much less to rule or bear
empire?"...

[Ambrose stated:] "Because that death did enter into the
world by woman, there is no boldness that ought to be
permitted her, but she ought to be humble...."

[Chrysostom asserted:] "Woman was put under man's power
and he was pronounced lord over her, that she should obey him.
and that the head should not follow the feet....Notwithstanding
that men be degenerate, yet may not women usurp any authority
above them....In the nature of all women lurk such vices as
in good governors are not tolerable....Womankind is rash and
foolhardy, and their covetousness is like the gulf of hell,
that is, insatiable...."

If any man think these my words sharp or vehement, let
him consider that the offense is more heinous than can be
expressed by words....God...illuminate the eyes of men that
they may perceive into what miserable bondage they be brought
by the monstriferous empire of women!...

And now I think it expedient to answer such objections as
carnal and worldly men, yes, men ignorant of God, use to make

for maintenance of this tyranny and most unjust empire of woman.
First, they do object the examples of Deborah, and of Huldah
the prophetess, of whom the one judged Israel, and the other,
by all appearance, did teach and exhort....I answer that
particular examples establish no common law....

Wherefore, let men that receive of women authority,
honor, or office, be most assuredly persuaded, that in so
maintaining that usurped power, they declare themselves
enemies to God.[29]

As Knox anticipated, this _First Blast_ was painful in the ears
of many. He had somewhat protected himself from its reverberations
by omitting his name and the place of publication. This anonymity
was probably largely due to his desire to conceal from Calvin that
he had published in Calvin's own city a position contrary to that
of the person whom he generally respected highly. Also, he had no
desire to be apprehended by an agent of Mary Tudor, the queen who
principally motivated his treasonable diatribe. Ironically, Mary
died shortly after the _First Blast_ was published and was succeeded
by Elizabeth Tudor, a Protestant who would have been disposed to
welcome Knox back to England.

Some months after the tract was smuggled into England, Knox
realized that he had caused Protestants there great embarrassment,
for they were enthusiastically championing the new woman monarch.
But Knox was, as ever, reluctant to admit that he had made a
mistake. Rather he wrote: "My _First Blast_ has blown from me all
my friends in England....The _Second Blast_ I fear shall sound somewhat more sharp, except men be more moderate than I hear they are.
My book, as I understand, is written against....The truth which I
affirm is invincible, and shall triumph to the confusion of all
oppugnants."[30]

The rebuttal book to which Knox referred was entitled _A Harbor
for Faithful and True Subjects against the Late Blown Blast
Concerning the Government of Women_. It was published in London in
1559 by a learned clergyman named John Aylmer, who later became
Bishop of London. While conceding that Mary Tudor was an evil
monarch, he maintains that Knox should have treated her cruel

actions as "the fault of the person and not of the sex."[31] He
doubts if it is "contrary to nature" for a woman to rule. That
women commonly lack leadership qualifications is due to their
upbringing. Moreover, he states: "We see by many examples that
by the whole consent of nations, by the ordinance of God, and
order of law, women have reigned and those not a few, and it was
thought not against nature." He concludes his incisive criticism
by putting these words into God's mouth: "Murmur ye at mine
anointed, because she is a woman?...If I be best represented by
the shining ornaments of the mind and not outward sturdiness of the
body, why may not she have at my hand what any of you have:
wisdom to govern, justice to punish, clemency to pardon, discretion
to judge?"[32]

The same year of of Aylmer's counterblast, William Cecil,
Elizabeth's Secretary of State, reported that "Knox's name is most
odious here."[33] The heat of the queen's anger was felt by Knox
when he was repeatedly refused a passport for travelling through
England.[34] Although he had described all women in an abusive way
and had advocated revolution against their rule, he seemed puzzled
that Elizabeth should find him offensive! He attempted to assure
her that "nothing in my book contained is or can be prejudicial
to your Grace's just regiment." Knox refused "to retreat or to
call back any principal point" for he claimed to have no more
doubt about it than that God pronounced a penalty for disobedience
upon all women. Yet he expressed his willingness to defend
Elizabeth's position as divinely sanctioned if she would acknowledge
that God "contrary to nature and without your deserving, has
exalted your head." Also, he chided her for attending mass during
Mary Tudor's reign by offering her this advice: "Forget your birth,
and all title which thereupon does hang; and consider deeply how,
for fear of your life, you did decline from God, and bow in
idolatry."[35]

Elizabeth's hostility toward Knox was, understandably, not
diminished by his letters to her. Moreover, since the First Blast

was published in Geneva, she presumed that he was stating the general position of the Reformed church. Calvin, realizing that it was impolitic for Elizabeth to confuse Knox's rash position with the more caution doctrine that he and Bullinger shared, wrote Cecil expressing his disgust over "the thoughtless arrogance of one individual." He recalled the conversation with Knox two years earlier when the Scotsman had asked about the government of women. Some of the ideas that Calvin remembered having expressed then follow: "There were occasionally women so endowed that the singular good qualities which shone forth in them made it evident that they were raised up by divine authority; either that God designed by such examples to condemn the inactivity of men, or for the better setting forth of his own glory....Both by custom, and public consent, and long practice, it has been established that realms and principalities may descend to females by hereditary right." Theodore Beza also expressed his displeasure over the First Blast and indicated that its sale was forbidden in Geneva.[36] Due to his objections of Protestants, Knox let his First Blast be also his last, thereby shelving his initial plan to publish two shriller sequels.

The European Calvinists were quite ready for Knox to go home. From Geneva he moved northward to the French seaport of Dieppe, where he preached while awaiting an invitation to return to Scotland. French pastor Francois Morel, after observing Knox's rabble-rousing at Dieppe, wrote Calvin in exasperation. He pointed out that Knox's dogma that "women are unworthy to reign" was especially unappreciated. Morel also expressed this feeling: "I fear that Knox may fill Scotland with his madness."[37]

Even before the First Blast was published, Knox had given the Queen Regent of Scotland personal reason for hoping he would not return to Edinburgh. In a letter to her, ironically to request favors for the Protestants, he had called her religion "poison" and "damnable idolatry."[38] In his Reformation history, Knox libelously refers to Mary of Guise as a "wanton widow" and compares

her to an "unruly cow."[39] Vulgarity such as this prompted David
Hume to comment: "His conduct showed that he thought no more
civility than loyalty was due to any of the female sex."[40]

Yet, when Knox did return to Scotland, Mary was not vindictive.
She dealt with the Reformer fairly while holding firmly to her
French and Catholic convictions. This graciousness must have
amazed Knox for he anticipated that "beastly cruelty" would be her
policy toward Protestants. He was sure that she was awaiting "the
opportunity to cut the throats of all those in whom she suspected
any knowledge of God."[41] However, Knox was guilty of wrongly
attributing to Mary what he thought a Protestant king should do to
Catholics. Out of devotion to order and justice Mary had rejected
a French suggestion that Protestants be gathered together and
massacred--as was later done to the Huguenots.[42] She was much more
lenient toward Protestants than Mary Tudor had been.[43] When
Catholic bishops were instigating a heresy trial for Knox which
they hoped would have resulted in his execution, the Queen halted
the proceedings.[44]

Knox's furious preaching against Catholic "idolatry" ignited
a riot in Perth which resulted in widespread looting of monasteries
and wrecking of churches.[45] The levelheadedness with which Mary
handled the Protestant destruction prevented much bloodshed.
Rather than use her French troops to crush the uprising, she
decided that the grievances should be negotiated. Out of this an
agreement was reached that in exchange for no further desecration
of Catholic shrines there would be freedom of worship for Protestants.
Had Mary been a male, Knox might have come to appreciate the monarch's
genuine concern for her subjects. But Knox hated the Queen to the
end of her six year reign. When he knew that she was terminally
ill with dropsy he declared from the pulpit that God's retaliation
of the female ruler was climaxing. In his History he reports that
immediately after his proclamation "began her belly and loathsome
legs to swell and so continued till that God did execute his
judgments upon her."[46]

In his biography of Knox, the urbane Scottish writer Edwin Muir employs the Reformer's sexual stereotypes as a means for setting in bold relief the traits of Knox and Mary of Guise. This telling comparison emerges:

> If one were to accept the description of the sexes in The First Blast, she might stand as the masculine type and Knox himself as the feminine. In the battle between them calmness, self-control, reason, dignity were all on Mary's side, frenzy, vituperation and back-biting all on the side of Knox....He hated her self-possession, her patience, her moderation, for they were virtues which, as he was quite incapable of them, he neither understood nor trusted.[47]

Although Knox had assured Mary that it was impossible for a woman to reign with "a constant spirit of good government,"[48] her equanimity is all the more striking when compared with the tempestuous temperament of her opposition leader. Were it not for "the bitter hatred of the godly," writes Eduard Parry, "her liberality, wisdom, and good sense might have brought peace and happiness to Scotland."[49]

The Queen Regent's death in 1560 gave the Protestants the upper hand in the government. One of the first acts of the Scottish Parliament was to approve overwhelmingly a Confession of Faith that Knox and some other ministers hastily composed. It is now honored as "the original charter of the Church of Scotland and of world Presbyterianism."[50] One section of that Confession reads: "We flee the society with the Papistical Kirk in participation of their sacraments; first, because their ministers are no ministers of Christ Jesus; yea (which is more horrible) they suffer women, whom the Holy Ghost will not suffer to teach in the congregation, to baptize."[51] Several years later the Scottish government approved a bill declaring that women were ineligible to hold public office.[52]

Knox interpreted a law of Moses so as to give basis for prohibiting women to assume public authority. Deuteronomy 22:5 states: "A woman shall not wear anything that pertains to a man." This is the meaning of that law, according to Knox: "The garments of women do declare their weakness and inability to execute the

93

office of men....If women, forgetting their own weakness and inability to rule, do take upon themselves...the office which God
has assigned to men only, they shall not escape the divine maledic-
tion."[53]

In that same year of 1560, King Francis of France, the husband
of Mary Stewart, suddenly died. Knox writes of his jubilation
over this and then, as an aside, makes his only mention of the
death of his wife Marjorie which occured at the same time. He
states that he was bereaved at the death of "his dear bedfellow."[54]

Knox, in spite of his advancing age, was still interested in
consorting with women. In 1563 he was brought before the city
council of Edinburgh on the charge that he was found in a cave
with a prostitute. The burgh records do not tell of the outcome
of the case.[55] During this time it seems that Knox attempted,
without success, to wed Barbara Hamilton, the widow of Lord
Fleming. An unadmiring contemporary, Nicol Burne, writes about
Knox thus: "Being kindled with an inquenchable lust and ambition,
he dared be so bold to enterprise the suit of marriage with the
most honorable lady."[56] In 1564 Knox married Margaret Stewart, a
royal-blooded teenager. Knox no doubt was gratified that he
attained so high a rung on the social ladder which he had climbed
throughout life.

In 1565 Mary, Queen of Scots, summoned Knox to her palace.
She asked him to respond to the report she had received that he
had bewitching powers, a rumor which may have originated from his
forecast of the imminent death of Mary Tudor a few months before
it happened.[57] The Queen also informed her subject that inasmuch
as his First Blast was a broadside against all women rulers, it
was odious to her. Knox boasted that the tract was such a sound
piece of scholarship that not "any ten in Europe shall be able to
confute it." At that interview Knox patronizingly assured the
queen that he would tolerate her, as the apostle Paul did Emperor
Nero, if she behaved herself and subjected herself to the "true
kirk." After Mary affirmed that she was indeed faithful to the

true church, Knox castigated her for a conscience ignorant that her church was the Antichrist and a harlot polluted with spiritual fornication.[58]

William Dickinson, a careful Knox scholar, has observed that "in neither Mary Stewart nor her mother, Mary of Guise, could Knox find one redeeming virtue."[59] He accused both of them of being possessed by the Devil[60] and thus of having witchlike qualities. Those and other women rulers are, Knox held, "scourges to plague" those who are offensive to God.[61] Mary Stewart epitomized for him the "stinking pride of women."[62]

Jasper Ridley, in his learned biography, treats an episode late in Knox's life as revealing his "deep-rooted hatred of women" even more than the First Blast. Knox read a history text and fulminated in marginal notes whenever there was a comment on a woman exercising power. Ridley notes that Knox "castigates every woman...for acts of bravery and self-assertion that he would have praised as valor in a man."[63]

Knox concluded his anti-feminist career as a persecutor of alleged witches. He condoned burning them[64] and was personally involved in tormenting at least one. James Melville, a St. Andrews student, told of witnessing the execution of a witch in that town. Before her death Knox denounced her "from the pulpit, she being set up at a pillar before him."[65] Melville also described the terrifying experience of hearing Knox preach. Even as an old and sick man he was so vigorous that it looked as though he would shatter the pulpit.[66] It would not be difficult for such a respected orator to stir up mass hysteria over eccentric women.

Having now attempted to describe virtually all of the recorded encounters between Knox and women, two general questions can now appropriately be considered. First, what was the quality of Knox's relations with various types of women? There is a wide difference between the way in which this question has been answered. Most Knox scholars tend to accept at face value his protests to the very end of his life that his domestic relations were not scandalous. A typical expression of this position is given by Ridley, who concludes regarding Knox and Mrs. Bowes: "There was nothing physical and sexual in their relationship."[67] But it may be naive to rely on Knox's public testimony as providing the unalloyed truth about his private life. Here his own suspicions about others in parallel situations might be indicative of his own inclinations. When interpreting the social life of others Knox appears to have shared an assumption of Martin Luther. That older contemporary, living in a culture with comparable sexual looseness, held that sexual intercourse between a man and woman who are closely associated was as likely as the burning of straw when ignited.[68] Knox repeatedly insinuated, without evidence, that the dances and other social minglings of men and women in the Scottish court concluded "in flinging upon a floor, and in the rest that thereof follows."[69]

In Knox's own time there were Scotsmen who turned against him his own vicious accusations of others. James Laing called Knox "a lascivious he-goat" and charged him with illicit sexual relationships.[70] Alexander Baillie wrote that Knox, when accused of having intercourse with mother and daughter, responded that this was no worse than eating both a hen and her chick.[71]

Although there is no agreement over what intimacies, if any, were exchanged when Knox was residing with a variety of women, there is widespread agreement on why he was so kindly toward some women and so hostile toward others. He related positively only to those women who looked up to him as a supreme authority. Much of his interest was directed toward that type of woman; indeed, more of his extant letters are addressed to adoring women than to all men. Stevenson discerned that "many women came to learn from him, but he never condescended to become a learner in his turn."[72] Even though there were several meetings between Knox and Mary, Queen of Scots, there is no indication that he ever desired to understand her values. He was only eager to control her mind and actions, and was stymied by her unwillingness to accept his

dogmatic pronouncements. Hume Brown has provided this accurate
summary picture:

> Knox has no very exalted notion of the powers of women, yet
> in every field of his labors--in Berwick, in London, in
> Geneva, in Edinburgh--we find him the center of a group of
> women, whose admiring zeal and substantial support strengthened
> his hands when his hopes were lowest....From the letters he
> wrote them...we gather how humbly they sat at his feet and
> accepted him as their guide. To all interests and purposes
> he was their spiritual director as completely as any priest
> of the old religion. [73]

The second evaluative question is this: with regard to his
attitude toward adversaries, both male and female, how was Knox
influenced by his religious heritage and how did he, in turn,
influence subsequent history?

It is significant that Knox first appears in history carrying
a sword.[74] Although he may have never actually made personal use
of a lethal weapon, he incited others to violence. Ridley
acknowledges that Knox was one of the most ruthless revolutionary
leaders in history in that he proclaimed that it was sinful not to
kill one's enemies.[75] By identifying his enemies with God's enemies
Knox thought it was not only permissible but imperative to destroy
them by either legal or illegal means. Hence that bloodthirsty
demagogue "merrily" relates the story of the assassination of
Cardinal Beaton and praises the murderers of David Riccio, a man
killed because he was an influential Catholic.[76]

Taking revenge on cultic enemies was part of the biblical
heritage that Knox greatly admired. He frequently applauded Jehu,
the queen-slayer,[77] and prayed that a new Jehu be stirred up to send
Mary Tudor to hell.[78] Andrew Lang convincingly demonstrates that
Knox thought of himself as this new Jehu who "deliberately tried
to restore, by a pestilent anachronism, in a Christian age and
country, the ferocities attributed to ancient Israel."[79] Knox
had no doubt that he had a private hot line to heaven. "God has
revealed unto me," he proclaimed, "secrets unknown to the world."[80]
That alleged disclosure gave him the confidence he needed to urge

97

the populace to destroy Catholicism, "sparing neither man, woman, nor child."[81]

Knox had little appreciation of an altogether different religious theme, found in both the Old and the New Testaments, that good should be returned to enemies who persecute.[82] One wonders how he would have interpreted the words of an Israelite spokesman for God who says regarding the massacre of Jezebel and her family: "Yet a little while and I will punish the house of Jehu for the blood shed in Jezreel."[83]

It would be difficult to match the savagery of Knox's public utterances with anything recorded of his contemporaries. Muir singles out the Reformer's "inexhaustible vehemence" as his main distinguishing quality.[84] He was a trumpeter who blustered forth a call to vengeance. He played so few grace notes that it is ludicrous to claim, with Hume Brown, that Knox's spirit is "the truest expression of the mind of the founder of Christianity."[85] Indeed, there is little about the life and teachings of Jesus in Knox's writings.

Knox was a prime cause in subsequent generations of some cruelties against women. He and his followers had a sinister view of all women who deviated from playing the compliant role that tradition had dictated, regardless of how their extraordinariness was expressed. He, like Calvin[86] and Bullinger,[87] believed the Mosaic law was still binding which decreed, "You shall not permit a witch to live,"[88] and, as we have seen, he was actively involved in tormenting Scottish women accused of witchcraft. It is therefore no accident that it was when Protestantism gained supremacy in Scotland that the persecution of alleged witches became prominent. Anthony Ross states: "In the period after 1560 the pursuit of witches was to go to lengths hitherto unheard of in Scotland, as far as we know, and to be accompanied by tortures as revolting as any in Europe."[89] A Scottish law was enacted in 1563 which made being a witch or consulting with a witch capital crimes.[90] In 1583 the Presbyterian clergy called for a better enforcement of the law.[91] An Aberdeen churchman was commended in 1597 because he had "extraordinarily taken panes on the burning of a great number of witches burnt this year."[92]

Starting with the reign of James VI there were witch trials galore because the king himself was at the head of the hunt. That young Scottish king, who had been tutored by Knox's disciples, published a book on demonology in 1597 which shows that he accepted the wildest stories about witches. He explained why 95% of the witches are women: "That sex is frailer than man is, so it is easier to be entrapped in these gross snares of the Devil, as was over well proved to be true by the serpent's deceiving of Eve."[93] James' prejudices coincided with those of Knox in that judgment and in his conviction that the "Papists" are demon possessed.[94] James asserted that even children who are convicted of witchcraft ought to be put to death.[95]

Prosecutions were heaviest in Scotland during these three periods: 1590-1597, 1640-1650, and in 1660-1663.[96] In Fife shire alone 30 women were executed for witchcraft in 1643. One ghastly Fife record itemizes ten loads of coal and one barrel of tar purchased for burning one batch of witches. The height of this frenzy was in 1661 when about 120 women were condemned and executed for witchcraft. In 1735, when the Scottish witchcraft statute was repealed, some of Knox's followers protested because they believed that the government was in violation of "the express law of God."[97]

When James succeeded Queen Elizabeth in 1603, he intensified witch hunts in England. Historian George Trevelyan has written:

> The skeptical Elizabeth, perhaps with some pity for her sex, had refused to yield when the pamphlet press called on the government to enact fiercer laws "not suffering a witch to live." The outburst came with the accession of a Scottish King, who, though he rejected the best part of the spirit of Knox, was crazed beyond his English subjects with the witchmania of Scotland and the continent. His first Parliament enacted new death-laws.[98]

Encouraged by this governmental stance on witchcraft, a number of Puritan leaders in Old and New England were strong in their denunciations of witches during the seventeenth century. "To James' statute or to its colonial echoes," George Burr observes, "all witches later brought to trial in England or New England owed their fate."[99] The Westminister Assembly in 1645, at a time when Scottish Presbyterian influence was at its height in England, gave reasons why even harmless witches must be executed.[100] Between 1645 and 1647 Presbyterian "Witchfinder General" Matthew Hopkins sent 200 witches to the gallows.[101]

The American Puritan leaders were greatly influenced by William Perkins, a Reformed clergyman who wrote a lengthy treatise on witchcraft about the time that King James composed his book on the same subject. Perkins expressed similar reasoning to that of the king as to why most witches were women. Perkins stated: "Woman being the weaker sex is sooner entangled by the Devil's illusions with damnable art than man." Beginning with Eve, he went on to say, the Devil has found in women his "easiest entrance and best entertainment."[102] He even argued that "death is the just and deserved portion of the good witch" who claims to have powers to cure illness, regardless of whether she repents of that claim.[103]

At the time of the witch prosecutions in Salem, Massachusetts, Increase Mather asked the court to follow Perkins' guidelines. That President of Harvard wrote: "It is a grave and good advice which he gives in his Discourse of Witchcrafts."[104] Given this dreadful Reformed heritage on the Satan-seduced woman, that in no small measure streamed from Knox's vituperative tongue, it is not surprising that there were executions for witchcraft in New England. What is amazing is that so few were there put to death in comparison to the countless hundreds of atrocities in Britain during the preceding century.

Knox has been, and continues to be, a heroic figure for many. John Milton admired his advocacy of rebellion against monarchs and

of putting to death those presumed to be wicked.[105] Milton was
confronted with male monarchs, so the strong anti-feminist conviction that he shared with Knox did not surface in this context.
Thomas Carlyle, in his famous book on heroes, calls Knox "the
bravest of all Scotchmen" and "among the truest of men." From
Knox's intolerance we can learn, Carlyle believes, that "we are
here to resist, to control and vanquish." Carlyle defends Knox's
harshness against Mary Tudor by this maxim: "Better that women
weep than that bearded men be forced to weep."[106] Carlyle formed
his opinion of Knox, as many others have, by accepting uncritically
what the author of The History of the Reformation in Scotland
wrote about himself. According to that book Knox was the colossus
who was at the center of most important actions of his day and,
with little assistance, transformed Scotland from idolatry to
Christianity.

By contrast, Knox is mentioned only twice in the 750 letters
of Mary Queen of Scots.[107] Impartial historians are unlikely to
conclude that Knox had an indispensable role in reforming the
Scottish church. Could not the Reformed movement, which was
started in Scotland by the gentle George Wishart, have spread
better the authentic Gospel in English-speaking countries if Knox
had never lived?

In our generation every few years another adoring biography
about Knox is published. For instance, Elizabeth Whitley concludes her popular treatment in this manner: "Democracy...is the
inescapable legacy to us all of our father in God...who was con-
tent to be known as plain Mr. Knox."[108] Surely that Scotswoman
must realize that her half of the human gender would be excluded
from any participation in a Knox sanctioned government. Also,
Lord Eustace Percy commends Knox because he "blurt out what all
men think" about women in government![109]

It is embarrassing for me to present this study on Knox. As
a Presbyterian whose highest degree comes from Knox's University
of St. Andrews, I have proudly inherited a tradition which acclaims

101

Knox, along with John Witherspoon and other Scotsmen, as among the great saints of the church. Yet, as a result of this research, I now see him as one who was largely devoted to fanning the flames of hateful fanatics. Had it not been for that bigot, Queen Elizabeth and the Anglican Church might have endorsed more Presbyterian doctrine and the Scots might have found enough of the Anglican practices acceptable to join in a united Protestant church.

The long shadow of Knox is now seen in Northern Ireland and elsewhere. If the dominant Presbyterian Church there had not exalted one who thought that the only good Catholics are dead ones, would the centuries of antagonism between Protestnats and Catholics in Ireland have been significantly lessened? If Knox had not thought that the only good women are compliant ones, would Presbyterians have had to wait till the present day to see women selected for prominent positions in church government? Perhaps Carlyle's thesis should be modified: history is to a significant degree the march of villains as well as heroes. Yet the biblical proclamation that women and men have equal dignity and dominion as creatures made in God's image has become more fully accepted in spite of the perversity of Knox and individuals he has inspired.

NOTES

1. Cf. Jasper Ridley, John Knox (New York, 1968), pp. 13-18.

2. David Laing, ed. The Works of John Knox (Edinburgh, 1864), Vol. IV, p. 439. Hereafter referred to as Works.

3. Works, Vol. III, pp. 383, 366.

4. Works, Vol. III, p. 350.

5. Works, Vol. III, pp. 337-338.

6. Works, Vol. III, pp. 390-391.

7. Works, Vol. III, p. 376.

8. Cf. Patrick Collinson, "The Role of Women in the English Reformation illustrated by the Life and Friendships of Anne Locke," Studies in Church History (London, 1956), Vol. II, p. 264.

9. Works, Vol. IV, pp. 217-218.

10. Cf. Works, Vol. VI, p. lxii.

11. Robert L. Stevenson, Familiar Studies of Men and Books (New York, 1909), p. 312.

12. Leviticus 20:14.

13. Works, Vol. VI, pp. 513-514.

14. Works, Vol. IV, p. 238.

15. Works, Vol. VI, p. 11.

16. Collinson, op. cit., p. 261; cf. Stevenson, op. cit., pp. 314-320.

17. Collinson, op. cit., p. 264.

18. Works, Vol. IV, p. 245.

19. Works, Vol. VI, pp. 534-536.

20. Cornelius Agrippa, A Treatise of the Nobilitie and Excellencye of Woman Kynde (London, 1542), sig. Eviii.

21. James E. Phillips, "The Background of Spenser's Attitude toward Women Rulers," The Huntington Library Quarterly Vol. V (1941), p. 6.

22. Edward Gosynill, The Schole house of Women (1541), sig. Biii-Div; cf. Carroll Camden, The Elizabethan Woman (Houston, 1952), p. 299.

23. Corpus Reformatorum, Vol. 43, p. 125, as translated in P. Hume Brown, John Knox (London, 1895), Vol. I, p. 228.

24. John Calvin, *Institutes of the Christian Religion* Vol. IV, Ch. 20, Sec. 31.
25. *Works*, Vol. III, pp. 222-223.
26. *Works*, Vol. VI, p. 27.
27. Christopher Goodman, *How Superior Powers Ought to be Obeyed* (Geneva, 1558), p. 52.
28. Thomas Aquinas, *Summa Theologica* 3, supplement, q. 39, 1.
29. *Works*, Vol. IV, pp. 368-415.
30. Works, Vol. VI, p. 14.
31. John Aylmer, *A Harbor for Faithful and True Subjects against the late blown Blast concerning the Government of Women* (London, 1559), sig. B 2.
32. *Ibid.*, sigs. C 3, I.
33. *Zurich Letters* (Cambridge, 1846), p. 76.
34. William C. Dickinson, ed. *John Knox's History of the Reformation in Scotland* (New York, 1950), Vol. I, pp. 286, 291. Hereafter referred to as *History*.
35. *Works*, Vol. VI, pp. 48-50; *History*, Vol. I, p. 285.
36. Works, Vol. IV, pp. 357-358.
37. *Corpus Reformatorium*, Vol. 45, p. 541.
38. *Works*, Vol. IV, pp. 78, 81.
39. *History*, Vol. I, pp. 79, 116.
40. David Hume, *History of England* (Boston, 1854), Vol. III, p. 411.
41. *History*, Vol. I, pp. 118, 163.
42. Cf. Andrew Lang, *John Knox and the Reformation* (London, 1905), p. 60.
43. Cf. Ridley, *op. cit.*, pp. 222, 226, 248.
44. *Ibid.*, p. 231.
45. *History*, Vol. I, pp. 161-162.
46. *Ibid.*, Vol. I, p. 319.
47. Edwin Muir, *John Knox* (New York, 1929), pp. 165, 212.
48. *Works*, Vol. IV, p. 452.
49. Eduard Parry, *The Persecution of Mary Stewart* (New York, 1931), p. 48.

50. The Proposed Book of Confessions of the Presbyterian Church in the United States (Atlanta, 1976), p. 212.

51. History, Vol. II, p. 269.

52. Cf. Ridley, op. cit., p. 477.

53. Works, Vol. IV, p. 228.

54. History, Vol. I, p. 351.

55. Cf. Ridley, op. cit., p. 417.

56. Nicol Burne, Disputation concerning the Controversed Heads of Religion (Paris, 1581), p. 143.

57. Works, Vol. IV, p. 420.

58. History, Vol. II, pp. 13-17.

59. History, Vol. I, p. lxxiii.

60. History, Vol. I, p. 159; Vol. II, p. iii.

61. History, Vol. II, p. 159.

62. History, Vol. II, p. 77.

63. Ridley, op. cit., p. 475.

64. History, Vol. II, pp. 79, 85-86, 150.

65. The Autobiography and Diary of Mr. James Melville (Edinburgh, 1842), p. 58.

66. Cf. Ridley, op. cit., p. 503.

67. Ibid., p. 137.

68. J. Atkinson, ed. Luther's Works (Philadelphia, 1966), Vol. XLIV,

69. History, Vol. II, pp. 68-69, 102; cf. Antonia Fraser, Mary Queen of Scots (London, 1969), p. 204.

70. James Laing, De Vita et Moribus atque Rebus Gestis Haereticorum nostri temporis (Paris, 1581), pp. 113-114.

71. Alexander Baillie, A True Information of the Unhallowed Offspring, Progress and Impoisoned Fruits of our Scottish Calvinian Gospel and Gospellers (Würzburg, 1628), pp. 40-41.

72. Stevenson, op. cit., p. 322.

73. Brown, op. cit., Vol. I, p. 294.

74. History, Vol. I, p. 69.

75. Ridley, op. cit., p. 527.

76. History, Vol. I, pp. 79, 112.

77. _History_, Vol. II, p. 114, 124; _Works_, Vol. III, p. 183.

78. _Works_, Vol. III, p. 308; cf. pp. 245, 247.

79. Lang, _op. cit._, pp. 44-51, 245.

80. _Works_, Vol. VI, p. 229.

81. _History_, Vol. II, p. 121; cp. 2 Kings 9:17-10:14.

82. Proverbs 25:21; Matthew 5:44.

83. Hosea 1:4.

84. Muir, _op. cit._, p. 302.

85. Brown, _op. cit._, Vol. II, p. 297.

86. John Calvin, _Opera_ (Brunswick, 1886), Vol. XXX, pp. 631-632.
    There were no executions of so-called witches in Geneva before
    the Reformation, but 150 were burnt there in the sixteenth
    century. Cf. George L. Burr, _New England's Place in the
    History of Witchcraft_ (New York, 1911), p. 15. Regarding
    witch executions during Calvin's heyday in his city of 16,000,
    Preserved Smith writes: "In Geneva, under Calvin, 34 women
    were burned or quartered for the crime in the year 1545" (_The
    Age of the Reformation_ (New York, 1920), p. 656.)

87. Henry Bullinger, _The Decades_ (Cambridge, 1850), pp. 232, 236.

88. Exodus 22:18.

89. David McRoberts, ed. _Essays on the Scottish Reformation_
    (Glasgow, 1962), p. 398.

90. Cf. Oliver M. Hueffer, _The Book of Witches_ (London, 1908),
    pp. 241-242.

91. Cf. George L. Kittredge, _Witchcraft in Old and New England_
    (New York, 1929), p. 278.

92. _Extracts from the Burgh Records of Aberdeen_ 1570-1625 (1848),
    p. 155.

93. James VI, _Daemonology_ (Edinburgh, 1597), Book II, Ch. 5.

94. James VI, _op. cit._ Book III, Ch. 4.

95. _Ibid._, Ch. 6.

96. Cf. Kittredge, _op. cit._, p. 278.

97. Cf. Hueffer, _op. cit._, pp. 242, 247, 251-252.

98. George M. Trevelyan, _England under the Stuarts_ (London, 1904), p. 32.

99. Burr, op. cit., p. 24.

100. Annotations upon all the Books of the Old and New Testament (London, 1657), Vol. I, Comment on Ex. 22:18.

101. Cf. Kittredge, op. cit., p. 331.

102. Cf. Cotton Mather, Magnalia Christi Americana (New York, 1852), Vol. II, p. 41.

103. William Perkins, A Discourse on the Damned Art of Witchcraft (Cambridge, 1610), pp. 168, 174, 251, 253, 256.

104. Increase Mather, "Cases of Conscience Concerning Witchcraft," in The Wonders of the Invisible World (London, 1862), p. 283.

105. Cf. John Milton, "The Tenure of Kings and Magistrates," Complete Prose Works (New Haven, 1962), Vol. III, pp. 224, 248.

106. Thomas Carlyle, On Heroes, Hero-Worship, and the Heroic in History (Boston, 1913), pp. 158-159, 161.

107. Cf. Ridley, op. cit., p. 522.

108. Elizabeth Whitley, Plain Mr. Knox (Richmond, 1960), p. 220.

109. Eustace Percy, John Knox (Richmond, 1965), p. 218.

CHAPTER 5

JOHN DONNE ON MARITAL UNION

In 1572, the year of John Knox's death, John Donne was born
in London. Although both Johns grew up as Roman Catholics, had
many intimacies with women, and ended their careers as influential
preachers, the similarities between these men go but little further.

Donne has generally been remembered more as a poet than as a
theologian even though he was, as a chaplain to King James, a
leading figure in the early years of the Anglican Church. In the
past, any who might have hungered for a full Donne understanding
have been hampered by the piecemeal approaches of the literary
dons, on the one hand, who are only interested in publishing and
discussing some delicious lyrics of "Jack Donne" or, on the other
hand, of the clergymen whose taste is confined to the later prose
works of "Dr. Donne." But now readers can feast on the entire
range of Donne's diverse writings since they are easily accessible
in quality editions. Izaak Walton concluded his biography of
Donne with a prophecy that has at last been fulfilled. That
member of the congregation of St. Paul's Cathedral in London
predicted that the "dust" of his deceased minister would be
"reanimated." Judging from scholarly publications, more people
are studying Donne in the present day than in any of the many
generations since he lived. In the past four decades there has
probably been more written about his poetry and prose than in the
previous four centuries.

In spite of the thousands of essays listed in the bibliographical
books on Donne,[1] apparently no one has scrutinized his poems,
letters, sermons, and the Walton biography to find his outlook on
marriage. This long neglected topic should be examined as it was
one of Donne's paramount concerns. Hence this study is the result
of gleaning widely among the relevant primary sources with this
question in mind: how did Donne's attitude toward sex and
marriage evolve during his lifetime?

109

The three periods of his life can best be separated by its
two most momentous events--his marriage to Anne More and her death.
This divides his adult life into segments of about fifteen years
each: 1585-1600, 1601-1617, and 1618-1631. His years as a
bachelor, as a husband, and as a widower will be treated in
sequence.

Richard Baker, who had known Donne early in life, referred to
him as "a great visitor of ladies" yet "not dissolute."[2] He
pictures the young Donne as a man-about-town but not exceptionally
dissipated. Augustus Jessop, who wrote a scholarly nineteenth
century biography of Donne, suggests that he was an Elizabethan
swinger: "He threw himself into the amusements and frivolities of
the court with all the glee of youth."[3] In R. C. Bald's recent
definitive biography, the young Donne is described as an affluent,
well-educated Londoner with mild religious convictions and conventional sixteenth century morality.[4] Donne admitted later in life
that his pursuit of pleasure involved sexual promiscuity. When
discussing Hosea's references to God's judgment upon "the spirit
of fornication," he candidly acknowledged that the prophetic
pronouncement brought to mind "some remembrance of the wantonnesse
of my youth."[5] According to Walton, Donne spoke of "some
irregularites of my life" which caused him to delay entering the
ministry.[6] This moral profile emerges: Donne was an unbridled
hedonist in the first half of his life and penitent Christian in
the last half.

What autobiographical information do Donne's poems provide
regarding his views toward sex and marriage during his youth?
Answering this question is complicated by two factors. First,
dates of composition cannot be easily assigned to Donne's poems
because they were all published posthumously. However, due to
Helen Gardner's meticulous manuscript examination, the poems he wrote
before marriage can now be separated from the ones written afterwards.[7] Her chronological grouping of the poems provides an
invaluable interpretive key, for it shows that the sixteenth

century Donne is distinctively different in orientation from the
seventeenth century Donne. There is a scholarly consensus that her
arrangement is plausible. Second, the poems Donne wrote may be
more of a portrayal of the general human condition than a
commentary on his personal life. Yet, the fact that the attitudes
expressed in some of Donne's creative writings harmonize well with
the outlook which he championed in his numberous private letters
and with the viewpoints attributed to him in the biography written
by his friend, Walton, makes it permissible to look cautiously for
a reflection of the author's own values in his poems. Unlike
Chaucer and Shakespeare, Donne is the first major English poet for
whom we have extensive corroborative biographical material.

Donne's "Elegies," inspired by the cynical pagan poems of
Ovid, afford graphic insight into his sexual outlook during the
1590's. Some of the poems, as Gardner points out, show a "brutal
contempt for the partner of his pleasure."[8] Seducing a woman was,
for him, a matter of acting on one's predatory impulses. After
the stalk and the snatch, the victim is sexually devoured and then
forgotten.

> I spring a mistress, swear, write, sigh and weep,
> And the game kill'd, or lost, go talk and sleep.[9]

After the plunder, the hollowed out person should be discarded:

> Chang'd loves are but chang'd sorts of meat,
> And when hee hath the kernell eate,
> Who doth not fling away the shell?[10]
> Transient sexual exchanges are judged to be more healthy:
> Waters stincke soon, if in one place they hide,...
> When they kisse one banke, and leaving this
> Never looke backe, but the next banke doe kisse,
> Then are they purest.[11]

Nature's way is also expressed in those animals that copulate
without permanent bonds:

> Foxes and goats; all beasts change when they please,
> Shall women, more hot, wily, wild then these,
> Be bound to one man?[12]

Donne's bawdiest poem pictures an excited man, lying naked in
bed, commanding his richly dressed mistress to strip and join him.

"Off with that girdle," "unpin that spangled brest-plate," "unlace
your selfe," he brusquely orders. The erotic explorations in this
"Mahomets Paradise" are described thus:

> Licence my roving hands, and let them goe
> Behind, before, above, between, below.
> Oh my America, my new found lande,
> My kingdome, safeliest when with one man man'd.

After the male dominates, the nude mistress is addressed in this
witty manner: "What need'st thou have more covering than a man."[13]
Edward Le Comte has aptly assigned to play boy Donne these
personality traits: "Frivolous, arrogant, sensual, irresponsible,
self-centered, and ambitious."[14]

At the turn of the seventeenth century Donne had an excellent
government job as secretary to Thomas Egerton, the Lord Keeper of
the Great Seal of England. The position brought with it membership
in Parliament and contact with the members of the Egerton household. One frequent visitor in that home was Anne More of Surry,
the teenage niece of Egerton's wife. While this "plentifully
educated" girl was being introduced to the social life of London
by her aunt, Anne and John fell in love and made marriage promises.
However, Donne had prodigally spent most of the inheritance received
from his father's estate, so he realized that there was little
chance of obtaining the marriage consent of her wealthy father,
George More. Indeed, on learning of the courtship More retrieved
his presumed virginal daughter to his country residence, hopeful
that separation would cool the relationship.[15]

Anne's father did not realize that a clandestine wedding had
already transpired. Screwing up his courage, Donne wrote to
"the Right Worshipful Sir George More" in February, 1602, and
commented as he broke the news, "I know this letter shall find you
full of passion." He explained that he and Anne "adventurd equally"
into a marriage some months earlier and that this was done without
seeking her father's permission because he knew that his financial
status was "lesse than fitt for her." Donne went on to express his
devotion "for her whom I tender much more than my fortunes or lyfe

(els I would I might neyther joy in this lyfe, nor enjoy the next)."
He reasoned that since the marriage "is irremediably donne" George
More should not "destroy" Anne and himself by refusing to accept
him as a son-in-law. He concluded the letter with a pledge: "As
my love ys directed unchangeably upon her, so all my labors shall
concur to her contentment."[16]

Far from placating the anger of Anne's father, Donne's
confession made him more furious. Donne had violated both church
and state laws in marrying a minor without parental consent.
To make matters worse, the father was aware of Donne's reputation
as a philander.[17] More saw to it that Donne was dismissed from
his employment and cast into prison, along with other members of
the secret wedding party.[18] Although Donne soon persuaded Egerton
to arrange for his release from prison, he was unable to convince
the Lord Keeper to restore him to his former work. Donne begged
More to consider Anne's mental anguish and "how litle and how short
the comfort and pleasure of destroyeng ys." He also made this
humble vow: "All my endevors, and the whole course of my lyfe
shal be bent, to make my selfe worthy of your favor and her love."[19]

Donne's persuasive approach was to no avail, because More
initiated proceedings to annul the marriage. Legal and physical
sanctions were needed before he was to accept the marriage as a
fait accompli. When it was validated by a court in the spring of
1602[20] it is likely that by then Anne was noticably pregnant.[21]
More was left with no respectable option but to turn Anne over to
her husband. However, More continued to express his disapproval
by refusing to give any financial support to his jobless son-in-law.
In a letter to Anne, Donne sums up their plight with this signature:
"John Donne, Anne Donne, Un-done."[22] At the same time he referred
to his love for Anne as "the sicknes of which I dyed."[23]

This unsmooth course of true love has overtones of that most
famous of medieval romances between Peter Abelard and Heloise.
Both Abelard and Donne were victims of vindictive guardians.
Scholarly Abelard lost his professional position and his masculinity

as a result of Canon Fulbert's rage on learning of the love affair
involving his brilliant teenage niece. That twelfth century
romance has left to history one element that is unfortunately missing
in the Donne-More relationship. Some passionate letters of Heloise
have survived, but there are no letters remaining to reveal Anne's
affection for her spouse.

The sacrifices resulting from Donne's marriage were to continue. Throughout most of the years that he and Anne were together,
they were in a state of desperate deprivation. To use one of
Donne's images, his taper of prosperity was blown out when it
burned brightest.[24] Without regular employment for more than a
decade after marriage, the Donnes survived largely on contributions
of patrons who appreciated John's poetry and companionship.
Having only himself to give to Anne, he pens these sympathic words:
"I write...by the side of her whom, because I have transplanted
into a wretched fortune, I must labour to disguise that from her by
all such honest devices, as giving her my company and discourse."[25]
Several years later, in 1614, he remarks about this costly marital
relationship: "We had not one another at so cheape a rate, as
that we should ever be wearye of one another."[26] Walton states
that their "mutual and cordial affections" made "their bread of
sorrow taste more pleasantly than the banquets of dull and low-
spirited people."[27]

The frequent sickness that also accompanied the Donnes'
poverty thrust them fully into the tragic dimension of life. With
regard to Anne's difficult pregnancy in 1607, John writes: "It is
the saddest lucubration and nights passage that ever I had." He
goes on to speak of "her anguish and my fears."[28] Again, seven
years later when both were ill, this is reported: "My wife hath
now confessed herself to be extremely sick; she hath held out
thus long to assist me, but is now overturned, and here we be in
two beds, or graves."[29]

Donne was in such despair during this period of social
banishment, economic destitution, and physical misfortune that he

admitted to having a "sickely inclination" toward suicide.
"Whensoever any affliction assailes me," Donne wrote in his
Biathanatos treatise, "mee thinks I have the keyes of my prison in
mine owne hand, and no remedy presents it selfe so soone to my
heart as mine own sword."[30] It is interesting to note that during
the same decade that Hamlet was first being performed on the London
stage, Donne, about the same age of the Danish prince, was carrying
on a "to be or not to be" internal debate in real life. Donne
grappled with thoughts of self destruction because he felt that he
had done little of significance other than marry Anne. In 1608 he
looked back on a past "halfe wasted with youths fires, of pride
and lust."[31] He expressed gratitude to God for his marital exodus
"from the Egypt of lust, by confining my affections."[32] Having
regulated his emotions by becoming a part of a supportive domestic
community, he also needed to feel "incorporated into the body of the
world." At the time of this crisis Donne could only recall an
unfulfilled life: he had attended law school but had not become
an attorney; he had studied theology extensively but had not
become a clergyman; he had engaged in creative writing but had not
published anything. Donne's existential anguish is given this
articulation: "I would fain do something; but that I cannot tell
what, is no wonder. For to chuse, is to do: but to be no part of
any body, is to be nothing."[33] He felt like a clod broken off
from the continent of culture, and prayed:

> Re-create mee, now growne ruinous:
> My heart is by dejection, clay,
> And by selfe-murder, red.
> From this red earth, O Father, purge away
> All vicious tinctures, that new fashioned
> I may rise up from death, before I'am dead.[34]

Anne's steadfast love during this time no doubt greatly
assisted him in rising from his melancholy to newness of life.
This is the way Bald writes of her devotion: "Ann Donne must have
had the perception and intelligence to be a real companion to him
and to share, in some degree at least, in his interests; above all,
by her steadiness and dependability, she compensated for his

mercurial temperament and helped to give him a sense of stability."[35]

The poetry that Donne wrote during this connubial period of life is quite distinct from that of his bachelor years. Gardner has observed that after marriage Donne's conception of love was "radically different from the naturalistic view that had been the basis of much of his earlier love poetry."[36] Value is now placed on mutual service and permanent union rather than on male titillation and temporary affairs. The metamorphosis can be discerned in a poem which may have been written to commemorate an anniversary of his own marriage:

> All other things, to their destruction draw,
> Only our love hath no decay;
> This, no tomorrow hath, nor yesterday,
> Running it never runs from us away,
> But truly keepes his first, last, everlasting day.[37]

There are a number of poems that reflect the mature love which Donne experienced with his wife. Several of these are worth examining carefully, for they contain the essence of his developed view of love. They are: "The Exstasie," "The Canonization," "The Good-morrow," and "A Valediction: forbidding Mourning." Clay Hunt's judgment of these poems is sound:

> All four of these works are poems of intense and wholehearted emotional commitment; they all insist on the uniqueness of the love, both in contrast to the love affairs of other men and in contrast to Donne's other experiences of love....These poems demonstrate such an internal consistency in their treatment of the love affair, and they express attitudes which conform so closely to those which we would expect Donne to have had as a result of the circumstances of his marriage—and which we know from his letters that he actually did have—that it seems to me virtually certain that they were all based on Donne's love for Anne More.[38]

The relationship between the mental and the physical components of love is dealt with in "Exstasie," the most discussed of all of Donne's poems. Herbert Grierson rightly considers it "one of the most important of the lyrics as a statement of Donne's metaphysic of love, of the interconnexion and mutual dependence of body and soul."[39] The bard has rejected his earlier assumption that love

116

is primarily casual carnality, but he cannot accept the opposite
that love is principally discarnate spirituality. A cardinal
conviction on love, which was to possess him for the rest of his
life, was arrived at about the time "Exstasie" was written. This
is how he succinctly states it: "I am much of one sect in the
philosophy of love; which, though it be directed upon the mind,
doth inhere in the body, and find plenty entertainment there."[40]
This philosophical doctrine has for Donne a religious fervor, so
he prays:

> From thinking us all soule, neglecting thus
> Our mutual duties, Lord deliver us.[41]

"Exstasie" can best be read as a parody of the Platonism that
had infused religion and philosophy for two millennia and was
especially prominent in the Renaissance era in which Donne lived.
Plato had differentiated between heavenly and vulgar love. The
latter is "of the body rather than of the soul" and is experienced in heterosexual relations. The aim of the good
person is to dissociate love from all physical contacts.[42]
Plotinus, the most prominent non-Christian Platonist, distinguished
between the pure form of love that seeks absolute beauty and the
vile form that is associated with marital sexuality.[43] Those
sharing this philosophy of soul-body dichotomy thought of the body
as a "tomb" or a "prison" from which the soul could be released
by death or by occasional mystic ecstasies in the present existence.

In tho first part of "Exstasie," love "interinanimates two
soules" in an ecstasy while the lovers' bodies "like sepulchrall
statues lay." Donne is here, as in later sermons, disdainful of
alleged ethereal experiences consisting of "the body remaining upon
the floore, or in the bed" while the soul goes out "to the
contemplation of heavenly things."[44] It was not the ascent of
souls into incorporeal rapture but their descent into a psychosomatic
unity which effects "that subtle knot, which makes us man." Thus
the sexual components of love are not impurities ("drosse") to be

117

flushed away, but an alloy which strengthens the bond. Incidentally, in this poem Donne introduces to the English vocabulary the modern meaning of "sexe" as conjugal intercourse. The rational soul, which in the individual corresponds to the ruler in the state, needs emotions within bodily parts in order to function freely. Hence, the poem climaxes in a "coup de grace for neoplatonic love":[45]

> So must pure lovers soules descend
> T'affections, and to faculties,
> That sense may reach and apprehend,
> Else a great Prince in prison lies.
>
> To'our bodies turne wee then, that so
> Weake men on love reveal'd may looke;
> Loves mysteries in soules doe grow,
> But yet the body is his booke.[46]

The "love reveal'd" to which Donne refers is the incarnation of God which is at the heart of the Christian revelation. "Weake men" need to behold those persons in whom the heavenly spirit and the earthly flesh are integrated. Hence, "Exstasie" has a surprise ending, for the pagan concept of ecstasy with which it began is transmuted into the Christian concept of enfleshment. The notion of flight from the body is abandoned because the blessed state is found where the divine is drenched in the sensate.

Donne's "Canonization" is an ode to his defiant marriage. He addresses those who have ridiculed him for following his romantic urges and thereby exchanging wealth and position for poverty and sickness. With a burst of exasperation he begins:

> For Godsake hold your tongue, and let me love,
> Or chide my palsie, or my gout,
> My five gray haires, or ruin'd fortune flout,
> With wealth your state, your minde with Arts improve,
> Take you a course, get you a place,[47]
> Observe his honour, or his grace...

In describing those who are obsessed with success Donne is also presenting his own self-seeking ambition that was strong in the decade before his marriage. Since he was never able to eliminate his desire for career advancement and creature comforts, this poem should be viewed, in part, as an argument with his own common sense judgment.

In the third stanza of "Canonization," marriage is interpreted
as a death to materialistic values and as a resurrection to a true
awareness of the nature of love. Like butterflies attracted by a
candle John and Anne were drawn together by a flame that enlightened
but burned them to death. They had lost worldly status but had
gained a new understanding of themselves. Their androgynous unity
now combined the strong and gentle traits of each sex: "Wee in us
finde the 'Eagle and the Dove." Thus their mutual self-denial is
a participation in the central dynamics of the Christian drama:

> Wee dye and rise the same, and prove
> Mysterious by this love.[48]

Lovers who renounce self-glorifying impulses should, in Donne's
opinion, be candidates for sainthood. Like the traditional ascetic
saints they do not conform to secular mores but, unlike them, they
do not treat the flesh contemptuously. The lasting monument to
those "canoniz'd for Love" will be well wrought love poetry, not
epitaphs carved on expensive tombs.

Donne concludes this first hymn to a new breed of holy persons
by claiming that others in the future will want to emulate those
"to whome love was peace." With respect to the serenity of love
which is here endorsed, Joan Bennett has written:

> Unreciprocated love is a torment of the spirit, but reciprocated
> love is peace and happiness. In the astonishment and uncertainty
> of the early stages of love there is excitement and there is
> also fear, but there comes a time when there is confidence
> and a sense of profound security. Donne is a great love poet
> because his poetry records and communicates these diverse
> experiences....He had felt almost everything a man can feel
> about a woman, scorn, self-contempt, anguish, sensual delight,
> and the peace and security of mutual love.[49]

Donne was quite aware of how much his marriage had contributed
to the refining of his affections. Thus he opened "Good-morrow"
with these sentiments:

> In wonder by my troth, what thou, and I
> Did, till we lov'd? were we not wean'd till then?
> But suck'd on countrey pleasures, childishly?[50]

The main theme of this poem is contained in these lines:

> And now good morrow to our waking soules,
> Which watch not one another out of feare;
> For love, all love of other sights controules,
> And makes one little roome, an every where.[51]

Human lovers, Donne believed, are a macrocosm of cosmic love. Paradoxically, man is to the world as a giant is to a dwarf. "It is too little to call man a little world," Donne explains; "except God, Man is a diminutive to nothing else ."[52] The macrocosm/microcosm imagery is continued in the concluding stanza of "Goodmorrow":

> My face in thine eye, thine in mine appeares,...
> Where can we finde two better hemispheares
> Without sharpe North, without declining West?[53]

In this striking figure Donne relates the eyeballs to the endless global earth. In the exposed hemispheres of the beloved's eyes is mirrored the quintessence of the world of value. When the pictures of the two lovers are spliced there is spherical wholeness. Donne perceives love as aimed at the restoration of the unity that marriage was created to have. The lyric's concluding couplet clarifies that seeing the presence of the spouse in one's self makes for the intensification, not the annihilation of individuality. The mystical oneness does not extinguish twoness:

> If our two loves be one, or, thou and I
> Love so alike, that none doe slacken, none can die.[54]

"Valediction" is given a plausible biographical setting by Walton.[55] In 1611 Robert Drury requested Donne to accompany him on an extended trip abroad. Recognizing that Anne's health had been broken by perpetual baby production and by the care of a brood of children, John wanted to stay with her throughout her eighth pregnancy. However, he came to realize that he had little choice but to travel with his patron. When he arrived in Paris he was troubled that he had not received news from Anne. He wondered whether he was "increased by a childe, or diminished by the losse of a wife."[56] He had a premonition that the infant had died, and months later he learned that Anne had a still-born delivery. Therefore, this

120

"Valediction" is a poignant treatment of the anguish of lovers who have been temporarily separated by the force of circumstances. Their relationship had been so purified by the fires of adversity that its bond exceeded even their understanding. Or, as Donne puts it:

> We by'a love, so much refin'd,
> That our selves know not what it is,...
> Our two soules therefore, which are one,
> Though I must goe, endure not yet
> A breach, but an expansion,
> Like gold to ayery thinnesse beate.[57]

Donne concludes the lament by comparing the lovers to twin compasses which trace out circles. While the one spreads out over a large area the other, erotically

> hearkens after it,
> And growes erect, as it comes home.[58]

Donne's poetic and prose writings during his years of marriage show that Walton lacked discernment in judging Donne's marriage "the remarkable error of his life."[59] "Love is a flattering mischief," continues the unromantic biographer, "a passion that carries us to commit errors with as much ease as whirlwinds remove feathers." Derek Parker is more perceptive in making this opposite evaluation: "The marriage of John and Ann Donne is on the evidence we have one of the most ideal and complete in the history of the institution; never was a couple more truly one flesh....There can be little doubt that his marriage on the whole was the great illumination and joy of his life."[60] The height and depth of that personal experience taught Donne more about love than did his wide reading of classical love poems or his rakish exploits as a bachelor. It is true that Donne's position in establishment society was "undone" by his marriage, but, to compound a Donnean pun, the mellow More-Donne love so surpassed his previous half-baked affections that the marriage could better be called the remarkable excellence of his life. Shakespeare's exquisite evaluation of loyal marriage is a propos:

> If this be error and upon me proved,

121

I never writ, nor no man ever loved.[61]

From 1616 onward Donne was well established as a clergyman,
but his success came too late to restore to his wife the economic
security which she had known in her youth. He was never able to
compensate her bountifully except by an abundant affection. Her
fatigued body died in 1617 at the age of thirty-three, a week after
the still-born delivery of her twelfth child.

Anne's death had as profound an effect on her husband as
their marriage had had. Bald states:

> The death of his wife marked a turning-point in Donne's life;
> it deepened his sense of religious vocation, and produced some-
> thing much closer to a conversion than the feelings which had
> prompted him to enter the Church. Until her death all Donne's
> deepest emotional experiences seem to have been associated
> with her; after her loss, his emotions concentrated themselves
> on the divine image and the activities connected with his
> sacred calling.[62]

Walton asserts that Donne "became crucified to the world" after
Anne's death and went through a long period of grief. Believing
that remarriage would profane his first marriage, he promised his
seven living children "never to bring them under the subjection of
a step-mother." He separated himself from others so that "he might
bemoan himself without without witness or restraint, and pour forth
his passions like Job in the days of his affliction, 'O that I
might have the desire of my heart! O that God would grant the
thing that I long for!' For then, as the grave has become her
house, so I would hasten to make it mine also, that we two might
there make our beds together in the dark." Appropriately Donne
preached his first sermon after his wife's death on this text
from Lamentations: "Lo, I am the man that has seen affliction."[63]
There is no record of what he said in that sermon but there was
recorded at the London church where he preached a charge for the
tolling of the bell at Anne's death.[64] Later, when Donne wrote
his most famous prose, "For whom the bell tolls," he surely must
have reflected on that lugubrious funeral. Feeling diminished by
the temporal dissolving of his uxorial incorporation, he heard the

bell as announcing that a "peece of himself" had been washed into the ocean.

The loss of intimate mutual love caused Donne to probe more deeply for its ultimate source. Some time after his wife's death he wrote:

> As the trees sap doth seeke the root below
> In winter, in my winter now I goe,
> Where none but thee, th'Eternall root
> Of true Love I may know.[65]

Donne deals more specifically with the continuum between human and divine love in his most significant poetic memorial to his wife.

> Since she whome I lovd, hath payd her last debt
> To Nature, and to hers, and my good is dead,
> And her soule early into heaven ravished,
> Wholy in heavenly things my mine is sett.
> Here the admyring her my mind did whett
> To seeke thee God; so streames do shew the head,
> But though I have found thee, and thou my thirst hast fed,
> A holy thirsty dropsy melts mee yett.
> But why should I begg more love, when as thou
> Dost wooe my soule, for hers offring all thine.[66]

It should be noted that the "wholy" in the fourth line of the above sonnet is a hyperbole, for even though God's love assuages Donne's grief in part, it is not a complete substitute for the love of his wife. Perhaps the "more love" therapy for which he begs is a pun on Anne More.

A sermon which Donne preached several months after his wife's death also focuses on the relationship between human and divine love. It affords an excellent insight into religious psychology and into Donne's own temperament. Several excerpts follow:

> That soul, that hath been transported upon any particular
> worldly pleasure, when it is intirely turn'd upon God, and
> the comtemplation of his all-sufficiency and abundance, doth
> find in God fit subject, and just occasion to exercise the
> same affection piously....So will a voluptuous man, who is
> turned to God, find plenty and deliciousnes enough in him....
> Solomon, whose disposition was amorous...conveyes all his
> loving approaches and applications to God,...and particularly
> in this text, "I love them that love me."[67]

That sermon concludes with a prayer that begins, "O glorious beauty, infinitely reverend, infinitely fresh and young, we come late to thy love." Donne also prays in one of the "holy sonnets" that God, like a young, beautiful lover, will captivate him:

> Batter my heart, three person'd God....
> Take mee to you, imprison mee, for I
> Except you'enthrall mee, never shall be free,
> Nor ever chast, except you ravish mee.[68]

Donne's sermons are often based on marital motifs from the Old and New Testaments. "Gods first purpose and institution," he asserts, is expressed in the Lord's affirmation, "It is not good that men should be alone."[69] This, the "last seale" to his first creation, discloses that "God loves couples"[70] and that matrimony is preferable to the single state. The fashioning of woman from a rib was to dramatize the mutuality of marriage: "She was not taken out of the foot, to be troden upon, nor out of the head, to be an overseer of him; but out of his side, where she weakens him enough, and therefore should do all she can, to be a Helper."[71] In another wedding sermon Donne has this to say about woman's place of dignity: "To make them Gods is ungodly, and to make them Devils is devillish; to make them Mistresses is unmanly, and to make them servants is unnoble; to make them as God made them, wives, is godly and manly too."[72]

On the basis of the Garden of Eden story, Donne criticizes the celibacy that had developed in Catholicism. "When God had made Adam and Eve in Paradise," he muses, "though there were four rivers in Paradise, God did not place Adam in a monastery on one side and Eve in a nunnery on the other, and so a river between them."[73] Monastic enthusiasts such as Jerome are denounced for their undervaluation of marriage. "Semi-heretiks" is Donne's designation for those Catholics who forbid marriage to certain persons.[74] Ascetic mortification of the flesh is, he held, an offense to the Son of God who was pleased to assume the human body.[75] Donne prayed, with Ezekiel, "Lord, let me have a felshly heart" and scorned "the halfe-present men...whose body is but halfe here."[76] Donne faults

the ascetics for their basic misunderstanding of the "mutual
relations to one another" of soul and body. He relates psychology
to vocation in this way:

> Consider that man is not a soule alone, but a body too; that
> man is not placed in this world onely for speculation; he is
> not sent into this world to live out of it, but to live in
> it....Though we must love God with all our soule, yet it is
> not with our soule alone; our body also must testifie and
> expresse our love, not onely in a reverentiall humiliation
> thereof...but the discharge of our bodily duties, and the
> sociable offices of our callings, towards one another: not
> to run away from that Service of God by hiding our selves in
> a superstitious Monastery.[77]

Donne expressed the outlook of the Protestant Reformers when he
states: "Roman Catholics ...injure the whole state of Christianity
when they oppose mariage and chastity, as though they were
incompatible and might not consist together. They may, for
'marriage is honourable, and the bed undefiled.'"[78]

Donne rejected the superiority of the life-long virgin even
before he became an Anglican priest. In an early wedding song he
tells the bride:

> Thy virgins girdle now untie
> And in thy nuptiall bed (loves altar) lye
> A pleasing sacrifice; now dispossesse
> Thee of these chaines and robes which were put on
> T'adorne the day, not thee; for thou, alone,
> Like vertue'and truth, art best in nakednesse;
> This bed is onely to virginitie
> A grave, but, to a better state, a cradle.[79]

Also, in one of his first prose writings, Donne analyzes the virtue
of virginity as follows:

> The extreams are, in Excesse, to violate it before marriage;
> in Defect, not to marry....Avarice is the greatest deadly sin
> next Pride: it takes more pleasure in hoording treasure than
> in making use of it....Virginity ever kept, is a vice far
> worse than Avarice, it will neither let the possessor nor
> others take benefit by it, nor can it be bequeathed to any:
> with long keeping it decayes and withers, and becomes corrupt
> and nothing worth....The name of Virgin shal be exchanged for
> a farre more honorable name, A Wife."[80]

Donne's most insightful treatment of the Christian doctrine of
marriage is found in his sermon on Ephesians 5:21-33. He faithfully

125

presents Paul's mutual submissiveness theme in this exposition:
"The generall duty...is expressed, 'Submit your selves to one
another'....God hath given...no husband such a superiority...but
that there lies a burden upon them too, to consider with a
compassionate sensibleness, the grievances that oppresse the other
part, which is couple to them." If husbands follow the example
of the gentle Christ their manner will not be "a tyrannizing, to
make them doe what we will."[81]   In the sermon Donne points out that
the need for a wife's submission had already received plenty of
emphasis in his culture, so he will say but little about that
matter. In another sermon Donne also rejects the double standard
that places heavier responsibility on the woman than on the man.
At a wedding he exhorts the groom to uphold the vow of exclusive
fidelity: "The body is the temple of the Holy Ghost; and when two
bodies, by mariage are to be made one temple, the wife is not as
the Chancell, reserv'd and shut up, and the man as he walks below,
indifferent and at liberty for every passenger."[82]

Presuming that marriage was the most transcendent of earthly
institutions, Donne often used nuptial imagery in his eschatological
descriptions. In one wedding sermon he selected a text from Hosea
in which an everlasting marriage between God and his people is
announced. That prophet held, so Donne believed, that God will
make the last marriage in the heavenly Paradise even as he made
the first marriage in the Eden Paradise.[83] Donne saw the temporal
union of spouses as a foretaste of the eternal union of God and
man.[84] He said: "Our Genesis is our Exodus (our proceeding into
the world, is a step out of the world)....Our admission to a
Mariage here may be our invitation to the Mariage Supper of the
Lamb there."[85] Donne had so much personal anticipation of that
final wedding feast that he referred to it in the epitaph that he
wrote for his wife's tomb. It reads: "To Anne...a woman most
choice, most beloved; a wife most dear, most pure; a mother most
gentle, most dutiful; carried off by a cruel fever after fifteen
years of marriage. Her husband, made speechless by grief, sets up

this stone to speak, pledges his ashes to hers in a new marriage, God willing."[86] One of Donne's wedding benedictions sums up the relationship between secular marriage and the resurrection reunion. This blessing is bestowed: "The God of heaven so joine you now, as that you may be glad of one another all your life; and when he who hath joined you shall separate you againe, establish you with an assurance, that he hath but borrowed one of you, for a time, to make both your joies the more perfect in the Resurrection."[87]

Donne points out that the Christian doctrine is not the immortality of the soul but the resurrection of the body. Although sexual reproduction will be discontinued in the deathless realm, "our loving of one another upon former knowledge in this world" will abide. The primary purpose of marriage as mutual help will be extended, for members of the more inclusive resurrected community will be "alwaies ready to support and supply one another in any such occasionall weaknesses."[88]

It is instructive to compare what the life and teaching of Donne reveals about marital union with what the life and teaching of Augustine discloses on the same theme. Walton discerned so many similarities between the early years of the two churchmen that he calls Donne "a second St. Augustine."[89] Before either took Christianity seriously their sexual passion was somewhat unregulated. Donne was personally aware of the parallel between his own sensual rompings as a youth and those which Augustine confessed twelve centuries earlier.[90] The similarities extend into their years of Christian maturity. Janel Mueller notes that Donne, like Augustine, "was a man of extraordinary sexual passion, ambition, self-consciousness, and verbal endowments, added to acute intelligence."[91] In the sermons which have been preserved Donne quotes or alludes to Augustine some 700 times.[92] The Dean of St. Paul's especially admired Augustine's sensitivity to human fraility and divine compassion. The ethics of Donne follows closely Augustinian principles in this dictum: "Only that man that loves God hath the art of love himself."[93]

The main difference between Augustine and Donne is found in the place they give to sexual passion and marital union. Augustine was convinced that knowing a woman was not an avenue to knowing God. He informs the husband who is intent on loving God that nothing distracts from that high pursuit so much as making love to his spouse.[94] Thus he addresses God: "What do I love when I love Thee? Not beauty of bodies...not limbs acceptable to embracements of flesh."[95] Augustine believed in divine love (caritas) as the basis of all good, but cupid love (cupiditas) was for him the root of all evil.[96] Accordingly, at the time of his conversion he committed himself to a life of sexual abstinence.[97] In doing that Augustine believed he was abandoning Manicheanism and Neoplatonism, but, in rejecting marriage for himself and for others in religious vocations, he was actually endorsing the paganism of Mani and Plotinus.[98]

Donne accepted marital sexuality as the crown of creation and believed that a spouse had more potentiality than a celibate for comprehending the many splendors of divine love. His songs of marriage are an enthusiastic reiteration of the first love song of the Bible: "This at last is bone of my bones and flesh of my flesh." Donne imposed no sharp separation between domestic and dominical love, for both are Emmanuel enfleshments. Whereas Augustine and his fellow medieval monks believed the Christian life required a holy asceticism, manifested in withdrawal from the worldly, Donne advocated a holy amorousness,[99] manifested in involvement in secular institutions. The English preacher exclaimed: "God forbid that naturall affections, even in an exaltation, and vehement expressing thereof, should be thought to destroy faith."[100] Donne was embodiment oriented: it was the divine imminent in the human, the religious within the sexual, the individual as part of the body politic, and the psyche pulsating through the soma that concerned him. He viewed the physically intimate and the spiritually ultimate as reciprocally enhancing.

This is how he expresses their marriage:

> The soule with body, is a heaven combin'd
> With earth, and for mans ease, but nearer joyn'd.[101]

Donne's greatest contribution as a poet-priest was his revival of
the biblical notion of the integration of spirit/flesh and his
interpretation of marriage as an incarnation of love.

NOTES

1. Geoffrey Keynes, _A Bibliography of Dr. John Donne_ (Oxford, 1973); John Roberts, _John Donne: An Annotated Bibliography_ Columbia, Mo., 1973).

2. Quoted in R. C. Bald, _John Donne: A Life_ (Oxford, 1970), p. 72. Hereafter cited as Bald.

3. Augustus Jessopp, _John Donne_ (New York, 1897), p. 18.

4. Bald, pp. 34-79.

5. E. M. Simpson and G. R. Potter, eds. _The Sermons of John Donne_ (Berkeley, 1952-1962), 10, p. 56. (Hereafter cited as _Sermons_).

6. Izaak Walton, _Lives_ (New York, 1846), p. 63. (Hereafter cited as Walton).

7. Helen Gardner, ed. _John Donne: The Elegies and the Songs and Sonnets_ (Oxford, 1965); _John Donne: The Divine Poems_ (Oxford, 1952). Most of the poetic quotations that follow are taken from these texts.

8. Gardner, _Elegies_, p. xxiv.

9. Donne, "Loves Diet," ll. 28-30.

10. Donne, "Communtie," ll. 22-24.

11. Donne, "Change," ll. 31, 33-35.

12. _Ibid._, ll. 11-13.

13. Donne, "To his Mistris Going to Bed," ll. 25-28, 48.

14. Edward Le Comte, _Grace to a Witty Sinner: A Life of Donne_ (New York, 1965), p. 57.

15. Walton, pp. 56-59.

16. _John Donne: Selected Prose_ (Oxford, 1967), pp. 113-114.

17. _Ibid._, p. 116.

18. Walton, p. 57.

19. _Selected Prose_, p. 115.

20. Bald, pp. 136-139.

21. Cf. Edward Le Comte, "Jack Donne: From Rake to Husband," in Peter Fiore, ed. _Just So Much Honor_ (University Park, Pa., 1972), pp. 20-21.

22. Walton, p. 58.

23. <u>Selected</u> <u>Prose</u>, p. 119.

24. <u>Sermons</u>, 2, p. 242.

25. Quoted in Bald, p. 156.

26. <u>Selected</u> <u>Prose</u>, p. 143.

27. Walton, p. 92.

28. <u>Selected</u> <u>Prose</u>, p. 123.

29. Edmund Gosse, <u>The</u> <u>Life</u> <u>and</u> <u>Letters</u> <u>of</u> <u>John</u> <u>Donne</u> (New York, 1899), 2, p. 37.

30. <u>Selected</u> <u>Prose</u>, p. 27.

31. Donne, "A Litanie," l. 22.

32. <u>Selected</u> <u>Prose</u>, p. 79.

33. <u>Ibid</u>., p. 129.

34. Donne, "A Litanie," ll. 4-9.

35. Bald, p. 326.

36. Gardner, <u>Elegies</u>, p. lxii.

37. Donne, "The Anniversarie," ll. 6-10.

38. Clay Hunt, <u>Donne's</u> <u>Poetry</u> (New Haven, 1954), p. 232.

39. H. J. Grierson, <u>The</u> <u>Poems</u> <u>of</u> <u>John</u> <u>Donne</u> (London, 1933), 2, p. 41.

40. Gosse, <u>op</u>. <u>cit</u>., 1, p. 291.

41. Donne, "A Litanie," ll. 143-144.

42. Plato, <u>Symposium</u> 181-182.

43. Plotinus, <u>Enneads</u> 3, 5, 1-2.

44. <u>Sermons</u>, 6, p. 101.

45. A. J. Smith, <u>John</u> <u>Donne</u>: Essays <u>in</u> <u>Celebration</u> (London, 1972), p. 129.

46. Donne, "The Extasie," ll. 65-72.

47. Donne, "The Canonization," ll. 1-6.

48. <u>Ibid</u>. ll. 26-27.

49. Joan Bennett, "The Love Poetry of John Donne" in <u>Seventeenth</u> <u>Centuries</u> <u>Studies</u> <u>Presented</u> <u>to</u> <u>Sir</u> <u>Herbert</u> <u>Grierson</u> (Oxford, 1938), pp. 102, 104.

50. Donne, "The Good-morrow," ll. 1-3.

51. <u>Ibid</u>., ll. 8-11.

52. John Sparrow, ed. <u>Devotions</u> <u>Upon</u> <u>Emergent</u> <u>Occasions</u> (Cambridge, 1923), p. 15.

53. Donne, "The Good-morrow," ll. 15, 17-18.

54. Ibid., ll. 20-21.

55. Walton, p. 70; cf. Grierson, op. cit., 2, p. 40.

56. Quoted in Bald, p. 251.

57. Donne, "A Valediction: Forbidding Mourning," ll. 17-18, 21-24.

58. Ibid., ll. 31-32.

59. Walton, p. 92.

60. Derek Parker, John Donne and his World (London, 1975), p. 39.

61. Shakespeare, Sonnet 116.

62. Bald, p. 328.

63. Walton, pp. 82-83.

64. Cf. Bald, p. 325.

65. Donne, "A Hymne to Christ," ll. 13-16.

66. Donne, "Holy Sonnet XVII," ll. 1-10.

67. Sermons, 1, pp. 236-237, 243; Prov. 8:17.

68. Donne, "Holy Sonnets XVI," ll. 1, 12-14.

69. Sermons, 8, p. 100; Gen. 2:18.

70. Sermons, 5, p. 117; 8, p. 94.

71. Sermons, 2, p. 346.

72. Sermons, 3, p. 242.

73. Sermons, 3, p. 242.

74. Sermons, 8, p. 102.

75. Sermons, 6, pp. 266, 270.

76. Sermons, 7, pp. 55, 59; Ezek. 36:26.

77. Sermons, 7, p. 104.

78. Sermons, 2, p. 340; Heb. 13:4.

79. Donne, "Epithalamion made at Lincolnes Inne," ll. 73-80.

80. Robert Hillyer, ed. The Complete Poetry and Selected Prose of John Donne (New York, 1941), pp. 286-287.

81. Sermons, 5, pp. 114, 117.

82. Sermons, 3, p. 248.

83. Sermons, 3, p. 240; Hosea 2:19.

84. Sermons, 3, p. 255; cf. Kathryn Kremen, The Imagination of the Resurrection (Lewisburg, Pa., 1972), p. 92.

85. _Sermons_, 8, p. 96; Rev. 19:9.

86. Cf. Bald, p. 325.

87. _Sermons_, 8, p. 109.

88. _Sermons_, 8, pp. 98-99, 109.

89. Walton, p. 77.

90. _Sermons_, 1, p. 238; 10, p. 348.

91. Janel Mueller, _Donne's Prebend Sermons_ (Cambridge, 1971), p. 1.

92. _Sermons_, 10, p. 346.

93. _Sermons_, 8, p. 236.

94. Augustine, _Soliloquies_ 1, 10.

95. Augustine, _Confessions_ 10, 6.

96. Augustine, _Sermons on the Psalms_ 31, 2, 5; 90, 1, 8.

97. Augustine, _Confessions_ 8, 12.

98. Cf. W. E. Phipps, _Was Jesus Married?_ (New York, 1970), p. 169.

99. _Sermons_, 7, p. 390.

100. _Sermons_, 7, p. 380.

101. Donne, "To the Countesse of Huntingdon," 11. 97-98.

INDEX